LORD HAVE
MURPHY

LORD HAVE
MURPHY

Waking Up in the
Spiritual Marketplace

Fran Shaw

With drawings by
Bruce M. Sherman

Indications Press

New York

Information about ordering books and e-books can be found online at www.lordhavemurphy.com.

Sources of Quotations:

Ch. 2 and 4 "This other Attention…"
– *Notes on The Next Attention*, New York, 2014
Ch. 3 "A quality… that compels attention"
– *Writing My Yoga*, New York, 2009
Ch. 4 "He who binds to himself a joy…"
– William Blake, "Eternity"
Ch. 7 "People who [think] they know everything…"
– Isaac Asimov
Ch. 9 "Whose dwelling is the light…"
– William Wordsworth, "Tintern Abbey"

Drawings: Bruce M. Sherman
Book design: Yuko Uchikawa
Cover concept and editorial guidance: R. David Shaw
With special thanks to Aubrey Paull

ISBN 978-0-9639100-9-7

Library of Congress Cataloging-in-Publication Data

Shaw, Fran Weber, 1947-
 Lord have Murphy : waking up in the spiritual marketplace /
 Fran Shaw ; art by Bruce Sherman.
  pages cm
 Includes bibliographical references.
 ISBN 978-0-9639100-9-7
 1. Life—Humor. 2. Spiritual life—Humor. I. Title.
 PN6231.L48S53 2014
 814'.6—dc23
        2013049043

Especially for Blake and friends,
and all the awesome millennials

CONTENTS

Preface

Murphy here. Seems daunting these days to speak about waking up without the words, Lord, smelling to high heaven. But it should be possible. We practice mindfulness. We get the big ideas. We are somewhat aware some of the time of some of our situation. Bodies with spiritual natures; spiritual natures with bodies; beyond spirit and body. No matter. It's not the thinking part that gets it anyway. It's something else, something that blazes up in collected moments.

We've read a lot of books by now, too. Writing about the Mystery has its dangers, namely, "putting-one's-hands-all-over-it." Also, "believing-in-the-one-who-thinks-he-knows." (Me, big-time. But I can work with that.) One toe in the ocean and I'm a fount of pronouncements. Holier than Tao. Am I so special that every trickle from the Murphy faucet is manna from heaven?

The alternative to explaining how to wake up is to describe the glories. The joy, the freedom. The relief. The pitfall here, too, is obvious. In the garden for a nanosecond and I become the Wikipedia of flora.

"Every flower opens in its own time."

"Every drop brings home the ocean."

See? Smelly.

Have you noticed lately that some of the words associated with higher consciousness have lost their luster? "Let's talk about Silence." "Let me tell you about the Unknown." Get my whiff?

How to clear the air? To trust what's in us and that we're finding our way to it.

Waking up. Heightened awareness. All of the unnecessary stuff dropping away. Feeling love, and connecting with our fellow earth-inhabitants. We know well that living awake is much better in every way than living totally asleep. We are grateful when awake! Attention mobilized, we receive something very fine that lights us up. We are momentarily balanced, vivid, juicy, spacious, patient, clear, free: we are home. Otherwise it's a stumbling and a mumbling and a hurrying and a worrying and a roller coaster ride or worse. Shine or whine. Chant or rant. Lord, have Murphy!

So this is my state. The pictures show it. My many states. United States of Murphy.

I'm moving to another country.

Hold on! I don't need to move to another country. I am not my state. Even when it's Hawaii.

I am not the landscape I see—am keen to keep seeing—roads, rivers, bridges, caves, inlets, outlet malls, amusement parks, barnyards. Butterflies in the field, bats in the attic—it's all the same to the sun when the sun comes out. All is lit. Lit is all. All is well.

Also, I may have noticed that, when I lay out, the sun is always shining! Must be there even when I go away from it, even when I'm occupied elsewhere with dense fog, scattered clouds, bubble highs, recent squalls, and next century's prevailing winds.

I am not my state. I'm from somewhere else entirely. I don't know from where. Maybe everywhere.

All I know for sure is that I love coming home.

Editor's Note: You have a way of talking about these topics that takes a little getting used to. I understand phrases like "keep seeing," "lay out," and "coming home" because I know you from your drawings and from the articles you wrote for class. However, we'll need to make sure, as you go along, that the meaning becomes clear to all.

CHAPTER 1

Lord, Have Murphy

When will Buddha bring the ice cream? I'd like the Instant Enlightenment Sundae, please, with no nuts. And could I have it to go?

I'm on the road in a fine machine with miles to go before I wake. I'm making good time. Many companions along for the ride, taking turns in the driver's seat

 whether I want them to or not. Asleep at the wheel? Yes, it happens. But I'm trying to pay attention now; my belly is full, the vista is wide, and the song playing is a favorite Rumi tune, "Swim the Huge Fluid Freedom."

Until that bump. A pothole the size of my ego. Boom. Down the chute.

Bad news. Red light. Bummer. A near one fallen ill. Danger. Inconvenience. Neanderthals. Expectations dashed. Venom spewed. A week on retreat that turns into Night of the Vampire Pain-Bodies.

And while we're at it, may I ask, who *are* all

these Gurus Gone Viral on my supermarket bulletin board? Reincarnated Atlanteans? I'm getting a sinking feeling. Books, classes, lechers, workshops. Weapons of mass instruction are proliferating. Taking us down the garden path?

"Dream a Better You." With Ima Wake and U.R. Nott, LLC.

"Bowel Movement Types and the Enneagram." Taught by Facebook-certified expert Laurie Satori. #powerupurass

"Here's the Map, Talk This Way, and Follow Me." Led by Lord Earnest Worthing, Top Dog at The Worthing Institute. #nailupurass

"Sedona and Gomorrah: Snake Oil Cures for Desert Wanderers." Sung by Crystal Trendy.

 "Morph with Murph: Guided Meta-Meditation and Ayahuasca Study Group." Tuesdays at 8. *"We have a regular group and a control group. Light bodies only, please."*

Murphy, teach? Not likely to go well. I have yet to learn my lesson that as soon as I think I can give you something, the only Something worth giving has left the premises.

Ed. Note: Lots of raw material here as you begin to sample the spiritual marketplace. Every line is packed. You may need to take it a little slower so we can digest it all! What do you mean by "down the chute"? Sense of presence lost? And the word Something capitalized? I'm guessing you mean the finer energy one experiences when awake.

Breaking the Law

Murphy's Law: If anything can go wrong, it will. New wrinkle.

Murphy's Law in the Now Age: If anything can go wrong, it will, to wake us up.

Well, hit me over the head, a "blow" does get my attention. A sudden fear. A violent outburst. A quick deflation. Bam! That sinking sensation in the pit of the stomach. "Oh, this again. Don't like it." But it may come with a toe-in-the-door thought: Is waking up possible even now, like this? And the blind man says, "Let's see."

Is that the sun blazing gold across the horizon? I hadn't noticed because my world has shrunk to the size of a kumquat. And is that a shining path on the water leading right to where I AM?

These waves that break over me, these bumps in the road… useful? Maybe even meant to be useful. Because it jolts me sometimes, noticing I'm dead-asleep, "identified" with something, hooked into it, attention not in my body at all—and so attention

Fleeing from the known

returns. Blessed nasty habits. My helper, my prod, my Murphy.

Whack! Smack! I must be pretty thick, or pretty lucky, for all these "reminders" that keep coming my way. But oh, beloved (in theory) brothers and sisters, can't someone make an app for when we're dead-asleep, that gives us just a little zap, say, to the third eye?

Dueling Downers

Not that I'm complaining but DISEASE, DISTURBANCE, DISTRESS, DYSFUNCTION, DESTRUCTION, DISGUST, DESOLATION, DERANGEMENT, DANDER UP, DREAD, DISILLUSIONMENT, DISCOURAGEMENT, DEFICIENCY, DUMPS, DEAD. Desperado! It was a dark and stormy night. But I can work with that.

Ed. Note: It's appealing to me that, no matter what you're dealing with, your attitude is "I can work with that." Now, what do you mean by "work with"? I hope that will become clear.

But sometimes I cannot. Things get impossible to control. The remote fails; the channel gets stuck on "Me Bearing This." Pile up. Traffic jam. Try to fix. My health, your health, fear, safety concerns, pained faces, planetary angst, fear, money problems, relationship demons, broken hearts, frustration, envy, doubt, self-pity, fear; insert your list here. Shifting magnetic fields. Yellowstone may blow. That asteroid is coming this way. Or has it already hit?

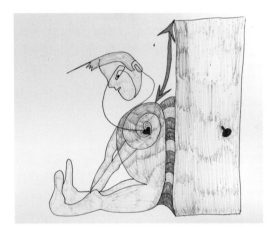

The uncarved blockhead

Exhausted. Fall down. Out of gas. Empty pockets. No can do. Nothing to be done. Murphy here. The uncarved blockhead.

Lord, have Murphy. Sacred Attention, have Murphy. Higher Intelligence, have Murphy. Light, Love, Lord, have Murphy, please!

The sun in the treetops; I happen to catch a glimpse....

Murphy, have opening. Have seeing. Have receiving. Have recognizing. Have allowing. Have aligning. Have joining with.

Murphy, have Lord!

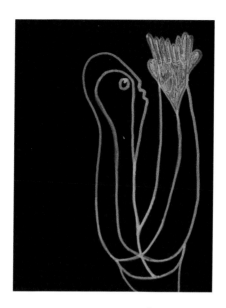

Receiving mode

Ed. Note: The synonyms for "Lord" that you give (Attention, Intelligence, Light, Love) help one understand your wider meaning of the word—not only a higher power but also sacred qualities one experiences when awake.

Your "aha!" moment (seeing the light in the trees) makes you switch around the title phrase, as if you suddenly receive a response to your supplications and realize that it's not just about help coming from "Lord" but that something must come from you. Just be sure to clarify, as you go along, what it is that comes from you (what you mean by "seeing," for instance). How does one "join" with "Lord"?

CHAPTER 2

Murphy, Have Lord

"**R**everend Murphy, may I have a word?"
"Quiet! Not now. Can't you see I'm blissed out."

Early morning at the beach. Walking knee-deep in the ocean. Sparkle city. Warm seas swell, steal my shins. The waves move through, the current moves through. So porous, barely a body, barely a Murphy—a vapor in the air. Wind tunnel for the Lord! Even when a cloud covers the sun, there is absolute certainty it is there. Because the air is lit.

In the flow

Lord AM Murphy.

So beautiful. Delicate. Exquisite. This subtle vibration. Leaves me speechless. Never want to be parted from it. There are no words—

Who behind the eyes that marvel?
Who within the ocean's roar?
Who gives rise to words so heartfelt?
Who the stillness at the core?

EVALUATION: No words? Well, maybe a little poetry. It's a start. Hard to capture a vibration. Definitely the clunky half-rhyme has to go. The repeated unanswerable question "Who...?" is provocative. If in reality (a wakeful moment) there is no "me," then... Who lives? Unfortunately, this kind of poem won't fly. The fashion today is broken-prose confessional or the grass-roots vernacular of "poetry slams"—(is that an oxymoron? like "spiritual progress"?)—as well as those bitch-slappin', fist-pumpin' rhymes of Master Wrapper Al "Uminum" Fo.i.ll.

Ah, the majesty of the ego. The source of so many great chart-toppers and slam poems. At this stage, whoever hogs the spotlight takes over, so if it's ego on parade, at least keep an observer in the balcony. My many Murphies. What a show. I never have to rent from Netflix! Will ego forever dominate MeandYouTube? Remains to be seen.

No worries, though.

Light flickering on the screen; on the sea; same Life behind.

GO WIDE, SAYS THE OCEAN, SAYS THE SKY.

My new bumper sticker from Glowaii. Yes, it's just another state, well south of the Great Unknown, but it certainly has its attractions for the esotourist seeking higher ground. No mountains need be climbed. No roads need be traveled. Nowhere to get to. Ocean as far as the I can see. Showering me with the right kind of ions. Just step in. Best of all, the sun shines steadily on everything equally everywhere— no preferences; after all, it's the sun! It lights me up. Frees me. Takes me into unknown territory. I can't make the sun come out, but I can lay out, make myself available to bask in it; or at least, in a pellucid moment, become sensitive enough to notice it on my skin?

But it does cost to fly there. Pay how? With attention. To give what is necessary at the gate.

Ed. Note: You say, "Pay with attention." Let me see if I know what you mean. "Attention" is one of those words one understands according to one's state. You're not speaking of mechanical attention that happens automatically (e.g. driving a car). You're speaking of two distinct kinds of conscious attention:

(1) "My attention" refers to focusing awareness on oneself here, such as sensing one's body, following

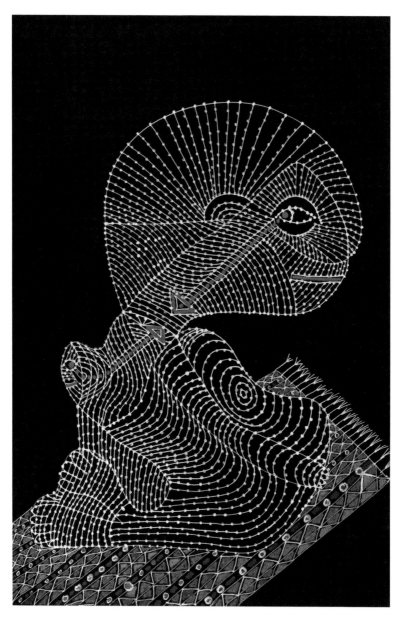

But it does cost to fly there

breathing, listening to the sounds in the room and the silence behind. Or like a surgeon present to every stitch he is making, or a potter centering clay on a wheel. Yoga class. One learns to activate this kind of attention through practice. To wake up, one needs to call upon this intentional focusing lest one disappear into thought and reaction. When one notices one is in automatic-pilot mode (sleep), one can call back one's attention, "give" it (your meaning of "pay"?) to awareness of body & senses now, and become present.

(2) "Attention-with-a-capital-A" ("the sun coming out"? an aspect of "Lord"?) is completely different—not mine, not in my control. There are no words for it yet many names—life force, finer energy—none of which gives the ladle the taste of the broth. Call it higher Intelligence, "this other Attention," the Self. There is the touch of the sacred here, so maybe use the capital letters to distinguish these words from our usual intelligence, attention, and self.

How are the two related? Perhaps when one focuses attention on one's body, in this atmosphere of sensitivity one may become aware of subtler impressions, a finer energy flowing through, a light around oneself, that draws one's attention; and so "my" attention "joins" sacred Attention. In the moments the relation is actually there, one awakens.

Bumper Crop

I'm back in my apartment. What a contrast. It's in Mediocrity City, near the Valley of Lowered Standards, in the burgeoning county of Megalomania (as yet only a small part of the great experiment America, so we can work with that). Renaming is trending now, and they're thinking of calling it Possibility City so everyone will want to move there. Once you've been to Glowtown, though, none of these glittering meccas feel like home. Am I missing the sweet spot?

Because it's all right here, too! Miles of inner

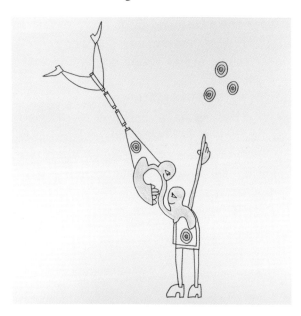

Trust what's in us and that we're finding our way to it

gardens. Breathing every breath. Red geraniums content on the window sill. Everywhere the sky. A good laugh tweeting around the globe. Flocks airborne under the moon. The young peacemakers smiling. Mountain peaks filled with silence. People's faces looking up. As tender as this breath feels, to be that way with you.

COME, LET THE TIDE RISE HIGHER IN US THAN EVER BEFORE.

Too long for a bumper sticker? How about this:
HOME IS WHEREVER I AM.

Sounds like code. Smelly. Maybe just this:
THE FARTHER ONE TRAVELS, THE LESS ONE BLOWS.

Because at least one realizes there *is* another way of being alive, even if it's by nature a coming-and-going in-and-out process that's working us. Brief periods of sustained attention and then Murphy can't quite hold the charge. Sphincter alert! Hold on tight! But that's not how it works.

Why is it one or the other? Murphy or Lord. Can't it be both together?

Ed. Note: To recap your journey so far:

Stage One (Lord, have Murphy) is about feeling the need to get free of sleep and break the hold of everything that happens and everything one thinks one is.

Stage Two (Murphy, have Lord) is about the exhilarating experiences of higher consciousness.

Stage Three (Lord-and-Murphy), then, one expects to be about moving out of an either/or situation into living in both "streams" at the same time, the ordinary and the higher, in balance.

I don't know if this is true for you, but I've found that certain physical activities that require paying close attention to the body bring receptivity to this other Attention. I could say yoga (meaning "union") but include in that term its many kindred cousins that bring together mind, body, and spirit. I'm not saying that awakening happens in yoga class or the meditation hall every time to every one. But there is that glow around people as they leave. Have you seen it? It may be this sacred Attention, going unrecognized and unattended.

When one finds oneself in a collected state, this Attention is there to be recognized. It's a daily discovery of something that one doesn't have to go out and get, that's already in one. Or is one. But you say you "can't quite hold the charge." Does it become possible to embody the higher energy?

CHAPTER 3

Lord-and-Murphy

Can I live Lord and Murphy together? Shall I ask Siri? (As soon as my iPhone charges.)

—Beepbeep—

"What can I help you with?"

"Siri, can I live at the same time in both streams, Lord and Murphy?"

—Searching…

"Lord and Murphy are one. Lord and Murphy and a bluebird are one."

"Am I in both now? Where am I?"

—Searching…

"Checking you in on foursquare."

Aha! Check in! Check in with myself! And so attention mobilizes. All parts equally here? Mind, body, feeling, balanced, and what else animating it all? Have a look.

Cellular Awareness

It's a new role for the mind, checking in. Activating attention. Bypassing the old programs. Finer energy inundating every cell. It's not my usual

21

Cellular awareness

mode of do-this-do-that, gather-information-and-analyze, but something else entirely: the sacred quality of *seeing*. Wordless, neutral, me, now. Present to whatever is here—and maybe what takes me away. Even when there is a reaction, I can stay attentive, so the mind remains free.

How is *seeing* "sacred"? *Seeing* Murph allows Something Lord to come through that can't get through otherwise. If my mind is occupied else-where—if the phone line is busy—how can the Call get through?

Texting?

Lord to Murphy:

> R u there? Any1 home? Cheer up.
> If u can stay, all is gimlet.

> Gizmo.

> Gibbon.

> WTF! Jesus crisp!

> GIVEN.

Checked out? Good to know. Now I can check in again. I'm a slow learner, so I need frequent check-ins to retrain my brain; the more I check in, the more I can check in. The focus shifts, and I'm not so interested in reacting to you anymore. And who wants to live a life in fear and loathing?

The second I check in, attention comes first.

Ed. Note: Can you define "seeing"? You say there is a sacred quality to it, implying that "seeing" can relate one to this other Attention. (It's good that you italicize the word "seeing" when used in this way.) What exactly is being "seen"? "Whatever is here" could be more specific.

For instance, you may want to indicate that one has a better chance of observing impartially if one focuses at first on physical sensations, such as one's posture now, the particular expression on one's face, the array of

Many I's but only one that sees

muscular tension held in various places. With attention grounded in the body, one has a chance to go subtler and deeper, "seeing" what more is here—other energies?

"Checking in" is the foot in the door. It's self-awareness. It's the instant one remembers one can wake up and "comes to." Useful. It cannot end, though, with "Okay, I'm here doing this" and then the mind goes back to sleep. Ideally, "checking in" brings "seeing," in which there is little or no commentary. Just wordless direct perception of one's body and, possibly, the finer energy (as you say) animating it now. Is that your experience? Perhaps make clear that waking up requires activated attention that "comes first" for more than a second.

Balancing Act

Nothing about me needs to change except where the attention is. Poised in between two streams, aware of both equally at the same time: Murphy momentum and Lord intensity. Multidimensional living. Great! I can't wait to try out these New Balance shoes and see if I can get on the bus running. Can these shoes take me to Lord-and-Murphy = normal, human, being?

Murph, you do-gooder, listen up. Serve the higher? How else can Attention come to earth except through our conduit-ing that quality into every step taken, every word spoken to one another? It's wonderful when two people co-inside.

Hmm. Not so fast. It's an exciting prospect, but what's the reality?

25

Ed. Note: I'm glad you're taking a closer look. Lord-and-Murphy, as you call it, means living in both natures, both streams, at the same time. A worthy challenge for oneself—even to keep it in mind during the day. Everything depends on whether there is actual perceiving of this other Attention ("Lord"). It's not something one can just "do" at will, this being aware of the energy lighting one up. Does it help to have a sensation of one's body? Maybe do an experiment. Be aware of your whole body, especially your feet, as you walk for five minutes. Then tell us how it goes.

Reality Check

Lord and Murphy together. In theory it's certainly possible. Other people have been able to. Great teachers and masters. At one time, they may have been just like us (except for the Pleiadians). There is at least a surface awareness right now (a shape in a chair; breathing). All there is? Go deeper?

Hold on; halt; must pause; for accuracy—which, apparently, to me, means: Stop!

Become centered enough to notice, for starters, that sound inside my ears and the light around my arms and body. It's wonderful to sit still for a moment, relaxed and quiet, so subtler impressions impress. But this is not getting on the bus running. This is getting on the bus as it waits for you at the curb. By the monastery.

What happens as I get up from the chair? Does

awareness rise with me to my feet? And skedaddle with me into the kitchen to slice strawberries?

Getting-on-the-bus-running seems formidable! Because often ol' blunderbuss is moving at warped speed. I need that app to be really mobile to check in.

I could do things v-e-r-y s-l-o-w-l-y, like in Tai Chi or yoga class. An excellent practice but, again, not getting-on-the-bus-running. In theory, L & M (how coarse; Murphy, you're hopeless) means equal attention for L and for M right in the midst of my everyday activities. Not the saint blissed out, stony as a statue. Not the animal pissed off, running wild, hogging the spotlight. Ride the tiger? Every sensory impression feeding presence rather than fracturing it?

Ed. Note: Let me see if I understand these phrases you use. "Getting on the bus running" suggests accompanying oneself with attention (even aware of this other Attention) wherever one is or whatever one is doing. By the word "impressions," I think you mean sensory data from all that one perceives, sees, hears, smells, tastes, touches, as well as internal sensations of muscular tension, breathing, heartbeat, posture, saliva, skin. Yes?

"Feeding presence" suggests that, when one is centered, sights and sounds do not pull one away but even underline one's sense of being here receiving those impressions. ("Fracturing" would be the opposite: attention getting dispersed in reaction to a sight or sound so presence is lost.)

An appealing notion, waking up in the midst of an activity without altering that activity. All of life, then, would be one's zendo. Have you tried this at the supermarket checkout counter?

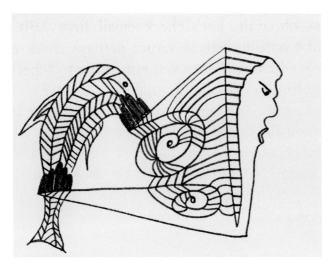

What's eating you?

Can I walk and talk and chew gum at the same time? Mostly it's walk and *get chewed up* (thoughts take me). Or it's obsessive thought-replay and *chew-on-that* (dog-with-bone mode). It's mind doing its mind thing, like the stomach producing bile or the liver making cod liver oil. No need to call it Incapacity. That's a city for whiners. I hereby rename it Ferocity. The town mantra is "Yes, you can!" Dog-with-bone, I'm determined to wake up! If it's possible at moments, it's possible for longer periods. You try; you succeed.

Lord and Murphy Together, Practically

Scene 1. "Preparation." Sunday morning, 6:30 a.m. Sitting cross-legged on the floor as the sun rises—oh, wait. Let's check email first. 7:30 a.m. Mental note to self: in future perhaps check email *after* meditating. Better yet, remember to "check in" while checking! Again on pillow etcetera, close eyes, sense, breathe, listen, concentrate....

Pop up! Wha' happened? Great idea for asdfafhaklkj. Have to write it down. Beautiful outside right now—go out? Meditate while walking! That's the intention, isn't it, Lord and Murphy together?

Scene 2. Walking. Heel-ball-toe, heel-ball-toe, heel-ball-toe. Disappear for a few minutes worrying about skdgkadghwej and sweoiuthbab, which, of course, may never happ—Oops! Heel-ball-toe. Knees. Elbows. Air on face. Bird chirping. Red flower! Scratch face. Sky. I just wish to be! Breathe. Whoa! You-with-your-head-in-the-clouds, don't step in it. Re-inhabit now as you move. But here comes Haskdhfja the Lemurian, who always creeps me out. If she steps on my toes again, I might just—*Danger! Ego inflation. Pain-body triggered. You are now emitting poisonous radiation. Like this, could do harm.* Turn around; walk fast the other way. But there's big noisy machinery bearing down from that direction! Caught between. Wait for it all to pass. *Wake up!* Hard to keep focus inside. Come into abdomen. Breathe in... "I."

Breathe out… "AM." Repeat. Repeat. Repeat—your only hope—

EVALUATION: This is not Lord-and-Murphy. This is reactive mode. (But trying.) Murphy circling the garden. No way in, if Murphy bails before the gate opens. (There's that gate again. What gate is that, by the way? The famous Gateless Gate? And who is trying to get where? My, oh, maya. *Who am I? Who lives?*)

Ed. Note: It's good when one knows what Lord-and-Murphy is NOT. As you imply, persistence is the key. One has in oneself what one seeks. It's a matter of becoming receptive enough, sensitive enough in a moment, to recognize what's there. I like the play on words, with the surprise word "maya," meaning illusion, and the abrupt switch when it occurs to you to ask the question behind it all: Who is knocking on what gate? The same Who that is on the other side?

Living Lord-and-Murphy

Am I awake? I must know. Sometimes I do know. Both natures, both here. Aware of a fine energy while just being me.

Are there signs? About Lord-and-Murphy—pardon my presumption—a few hallmarks, please?

Card #1: The subtle energy is the main focus.

Card #2: "Me-me-mine" drops away all on its own.

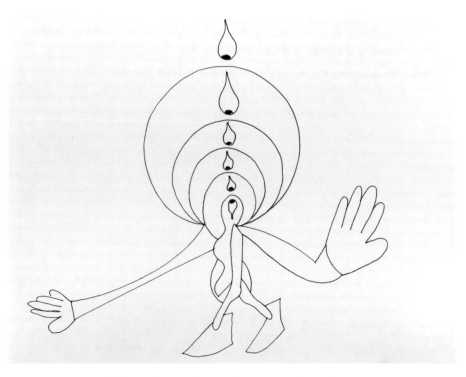

If thine I be single…. This is Murphi with an I

Card #3: The feeling may appear of being related to everything and everyone.

This is Murphi with an *I*. (Usually it's Murphy with a why.)

Heart closed, heart open, heart closed. Like a rubber band that stretches wide, wider—and then springs back taut. People as things in my way; hard to take, the unbecoming behavior, my own included. OR: Underneath it all, just people, fragile, tough, buffeted, trying. And a particle of the divine in every one (except those guys on the news).

When in closed mode, I should be nicer, I should be kinder. I'd settle for neutral. Or detesting the behavior, not the person. Like you love a toddler, despite the messes. Sounds good—in theory. But how

I should be nicer, I should be kinder

do you make yourself instantly feel a certain way? So I huff-and-puff to "accept" myself and others—good luck pushing that boulder up the Himalayas—all sorts of manipulationships going on there.

And then—in the blink of an I!—the discovery. Focused attention yields to finer Attention. Opening into light-flecked space where there is no "should"; so vibrant that every breath is not mine but Life breathing me; an energy permeating whose very nature carries the fragrance of all-loving.

Murphy can't "accept"—but this Energy can! A moment in it, and there is radical change—an altogether different creature here, for the moment. Wind tunnel for the Love! "A quality pouring through that compels attention—we are made for love—for a flowing through into the world."

Meet Lord-and-Murphy, human being.

(*Snap!* Was that a rubber band?)

Ed. Note: What a relief when one can drop the struggle and simply open to what one is. It doesn't matter what motivates one to wake up, once the threshold is crossed. When the subtle energy appears (as you so poignantly describe), one is totally different in that instant—and one knows it as surely as one knows whether it is hot or cold outside. The love you describe as beneficently "flowing through" includes compassion for oneself as well. Waking up means not only efforts to come back to oneself but what they bring: a moment of being actually related to something fine.

CHAPTER 4

Write It Up!

When all I notice are obstacles, for sure it's "my" attention alone that's here—and not "this other Attention, which *transforms*."

Is it clear, the distinction? Here the word "transforms" does not mean changing me or improving me but waking me up to a completely different level of being alive. Perhaps this sense of the word has gone missing for everyone except Book-of-the-Monk Club members. Sorry about that. It can happen when we writers try to sew something up from our Masters' silken bolts. Like good seamstresses and seamsters, we faithfully translate the Ideas into simpler language with plenty of relatable examples. And there are lots of us folks doing that these days. But why does it seem that the very Goodness of it gets lost in the stitching?

For instance, try on this eager vestment featured in a recent issue of *Elliptical: Journal for the Spiritually Fit*:

"Self is the nature of Happiness and Happiness is the nature of Self. Its realization requires efforts of both core and groin. Against all resistance, and in spite of that trickster ego, one pulls oneself home to the palace of Self.

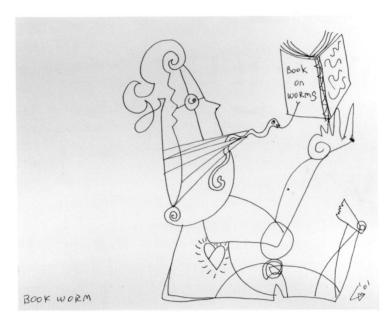

BOOK WORM

Down the wormhole

"When the mind goes out too far from There, only unhappiness can result. Then the mind must empty itself of itself, and gather itself into a one-pointed ball, and roll itself down the alley of forgetfulness into the hall of Silence.

"Seekers must mount their machines and do enough reps to feel spiritual muscle building, and so ultimately develop the strength to enter the gymnasium of God.

"COMING SOON: 'Working Out on the Stairmaster of Life,' climb, climb, climbing but getting...."

This garment doesn't seem to fit. Maybe it used to fit. Has the ass gotten too big? It's just that I don't think waking up means dragging dead weight up

Mount Analogue. I just don't think that's necessary.

Ed. Note: For you, transformation has come to mean at any moment being aware of this "other nature" and living in "both natures, both here." Waking up is not complicated, not a burden. In the instant one wakes up, no bags to empty or carry and nobody to carry them. And one can wake up often every day. One does benefit, though, from the practice ("reps"?) of bringing one's attention back into one's whole self just as it is, or else who is even there to recognize the subtle Attention and stay in relation with it?

Leveling the Playing Field

It's the difference between "about" and "from." Words that come "from" the Source, through an awakened speaker directly to you and me, go in deep. Resonate. Like a truth felt in the heart. Another level breaks in.

Words "about," we either like or dislike. Heady stuff.

Aha! So *that's* where the smell comes from! Getting "about" when you're expecting "from."

But writing "from" is a tall order for any author. This morning, he sits like a champ. This afternoon at the keyboard, he does not notice that he merely imagines he understands That "about" which he speaks because he so deftly summarizes others' "from" words, blending in his own—not seeing that there is no "from" left in them by the time he's through. But he goes on stitching things up with his own-color thread that's making it all wonderfully special.

Sigh. If I've learned anything it's that just because I have sensation in my pinky doesn't mean I'm awake. Yes, Murphy, that goes for you, too. You are special, just like everyone else.

Is there a level below "about"?

For me, it's when the writer makes "spinach" out of this mysterious process. Overlays explanations, concepts, diagrams, difficulties. Ugh. That's when I push the chair away from the table. No more for me, thank you.

Is there a level below "spinach"?

That would be "criminal." Rewriting a spiritual masterpiece and making hash out of it. Streamlining the words from an awakened one into a legal brief so the rest of us can understand them. Snake oil, anyone? Smelly. And not necessary. What we need is to be accountable to some minimum standard.

Every word from the real world.

Uh, can we set the bar a little higher?

Sorry to break it to you, Murph, but by that standard you're a pornographer. And what, pray tell, are these pages? Nothing more than another self-help MEmoir. And here I thought it was artful Self-display.

Ego usually gets a bad rap, by the way, in all this press. Why not pick on the nose? It can dominate at moments, too. Thankfully everything is put in order the instant Attention is remembered and can appear. Whether I'm strutting (just praised) or grumbling (just dissed), stirred-up ego can remind me of how far away I am from what matters to me much more.

If there is enough presence in me to notice a me-jerk reaction, sometimes I also notice that there is something here that is not in reaction at all. I'm grateful for that, because my attention is always in play. If inner talk starts up, it's a signal that I'm losing focus. If a higher level takes hold, all I wish is to continue attending to what is here lighting me up.

Ed. Note: I have the same impression of writers who, as you say, put their hands all over a sacred text so there's no more mystery or potency in it. So I understand your distaste for writers who want to be perceived as all-knowing; it's the revulsion one feels at pretentiousness and ego-display in others—always others. One rarely notices that one's own ego may be similarly engaged, perhaps not in display but in protecting one's image. It's as if one will do anything to avoid the pain one feels when slighted, imposed upon, or humiliated. Ever notice that a moment of bruised ego (a "me-jerk reaction"?) can replay in one's head for hours?

Of course one needs ego and personality to function in this world. Fortunately, this other Attention embraces all, and when one wakes up, one is glad for ego, personality, everything that's there—all useful when not dominating.

Owning Up

With my cupboard full of half-baked beliefs, I suppose I would be as good as any blah-blah-blogger on spiritual matters. You would, too. Apparently, there's a secret recipe for how to layer the cake:

1. Pick the Flavor of the Month: Let's say…

    OWNERSHIP

2. Begin with a juicy morsel from a better writer:

    He who binds to himself a joy
    Does the winged life destroy
    But he who kisses a joy as it flies
    Lives in eternity's sunrise

(Fabulous. I knew I could work that in somewhere. So glad. Let's read those four lines again.)

3. Research thoroughly (15 seconds on iPhone) the key word, learn about its Latino origins, and then use as a starter whatever strikes you that you can copy from the O.E.D.:

OWN, verb. First coined during the Golden Age of Queen Ophrah of the Isle of Inisnotfree. Muddle English *ownup*; from Ye Olde English *agen*; akin to High German *eigan*, Old Nurse *eiginn*, and Old Yiddish *oi-agan?* meaning "to be possessed"

4. Whip up some soul-searching word play about struggling with that demon ego:

What really belongs to me? Why do I think "agan" and "agan" that all things are mine? This feeling of ownership of spiritual ideas and states is simply ego reinforcing itself by taking what may be a transcendent moment and co-opting it. My ideas, my beliefs, my experiences, my attention. My head is spinning. Do I possess or am I possessed?

5. Sprinkle in some self-pleasing quotedium details of the day's little victories:

I looked down at the hard black pellets in the toilet bowl, remembering yesterday's long, curving, brown softness. Did both come from me? Are they mine? What's the lesson here? Which type am I, intellectual hardhead or emotional softie? Both? Neither? Too many rhetorical questions in a row? Keep going? How can things I call "mine" belong to me when me-on-earth is gone in 60 sentences? A mad dash, recorded on my tombstone, between the year of my birth and the year of my death. "Transitory" means "no permanence." What is real can't die—it's beyond time and birth and death. "Me" is not real! A light-bulb moment!!! Isn't one exclamation point enough?! Not a single blessed thing is mine or ever could be. Mine-ing requires a me.

And in reality, there is NO ME. LOL!

Voilà! Yum. Go ahead, Murphy, indulge yourself. Put as much frosting on it as you like, muffin, it's still nutty-as-a-fruitcake with a big glass of whine.

Ed. Note: You may ruffle a few feathers here. But one can use a little ruffling if one's interest is in waking up because it shows what is there. Ownership and ego are two great topics to go into more (I hope you will). Instead of living under the influence of ego, one can begin to live under a new influence. Can you say what that is?

CHAPTER 5

Higher Education

For what am I most grateful? Grad school. In
Holland. I had the privilege of attending the
Sit-Chat-Ananda Institoot for Lifelong Learners. A
state-dependent institution of higher learning with a
board-certifiable 40-year program leading to a Ph.D.
in Cosmic Consciousness Through Sustainable
Attention. I also got a Master's degree in Holistic
Lunacy (with a minor in Froot Loops).

The Institoot was unlike any school I'd ever
been to. A well-constructed building of several lev-
els around an inner courtyard that none were privy
to. Classrooms consisted of semicircles of straight-
backed stares directed floorward at intricate Oriental
rugs. After a few years, I even got to T.A. a couple
of classes—called "groops" there—and enjoyed, way
too much, the coveted position of instructing others.

Instead of a teacher, a groop had a "leder"
(Dutch anagram for "elder") and sometimes a young
"assistant-groop-leder-in-training." Instead of home-
work assignments, there were "taasks." Instead of
exams, oral "repoorts." For the first ten years, bril-
liant material opened up new whorls. It was the best.

My groop leder was the first awake person I had ever met. Working tirelessly with us. Opening up "hoos" and hearth. My tribe! I'm home!

Ed. Note: There is excitement when one joins with others who wish to wake up. You may be laying it on a bit thick, but with affection, I think.

Difficulty Has "Cult" In It

The next ten years saw a big turnover: lots of "droop-outs." How come? Dissension in the rank. Interplanetary tensions. The passing of many leders. Stricter regulations—although things always were very formal, in keeping with tradition. You had to come prepared with questions (no answers allowed), and you could talk only to the leder and only in Old Dutch, using a tentative well-modulated tone (almost a whisper).

Here's a sample, in translation, from the archives:

SECRET TRANSCRIPT G1208,
page 369 (of 2,857,144,285,715 pp.)
Last Century, 8 P.M.

QUESTIONER 1: I read in the literature that systematic study and purification of my psychological makeup will help me relate my unconscious configurations to potentially conscious structures so long as I divide my attention and simultaneously make myself globally aware of my physical body while counting backwards from 1000 in Sanskrit. But when I tried to concentrate like that a few times this week, I couldn't remember the part about the body. But I could do the counting. Was I just thinking? I mentioned this to my shadow therapist and he said I was definitely almost beginning to approach the pathway to the entrance to the outer atrium of the courtyard leading to the pillared walkway toward self-awareness. But I don't think I'm even in the neighborhood.

LEDER: *You bring very interesting material. You would like to become more conscious. You must find out what that means.*

QUESTIONER 2: [Gulp] My heart is… pounding… right… now… as I… try to… be aware… while… [Mumbling]

LEDER: *Speak in your regular voice.*
[Silence.]

QUESTIONER 3: I tried to remind myself to wake up by wearing a scratchy wool sweater for one day. It worked for a few minutes, but by the end of the day, all I could show for it was a rash.

LEDER: *You must want something very much. Try putting a pebble in your shoe.*

QUESTIONER 4 [Guess Who!]: I don't understand how to connect my lower flanks to my higher tanks so I can experience what I read about that others experience. When I was young, we had a dog, and one day my father... [five minutes of details]... traumatic. So now I have no authority over myself and can't make myself do anything.

LEDER: *Don't ever tell that story again.*

QUESTIONER 5: I've invested a lot over the years. I was a Buddhist, then a dervish, then a Fartist. I paid to have my chakras balanced and my aura cleansed. I've been t.m.-ed, reiki-ed, rolf-ed, and feng-shui-ed. Now I've put everything I've got into this one account, but my stock fluctuates so much, it can't seem to go up and stay up. I'm not getting back enough return on investment. When's the big payoff? That's what I want to know.

LEDER: *You pay. With attention.*

QUESTIONER 6: It is very important to me that I achieve consciousness and conquer sleep. When I'm in my life it seems impossible because of my... [list of inadequacies]. But sometimes here I have moments when I feel happy, like I'm really getting it, like I used to feel on windowpane or purple Osley, ya' know? before they cut it with speed. But I don't understand how that happens or how to do that on my own.

LEDER: *If it's good, I good it. If it's bad, I good it, too.*

Ed. Note: As I understand it, regardless of the different types of people there, the group leader's sole task is to "make them werke" i.e. awaken. Of course that person must be awake while speaking, related internally to this other Attention. Perhaps note that a transcript cannot convey how the level of attention suddenly can go up in speaker and listener. What is then perceived has nothing to do with thoughts, concepts, self-deprecation, aggression, or psychoanalysis, yes? Awakeness appears. "If it's good, I good it; if it's bad, I good it, too" looks to me like another way of saying "I can work with that," i.e. no matter what happens, one's response is the same: become aware.

Aside from everyone being asleep at the same time while talking about waking, or the assistant leder giving off the B.O. of a "stinkin' gooru," there was another danger: bringing up a topic that the leder might find "unmeet." For instance, if you dared speak about not liking how the groop was run (called "tilting at windmills"), you were threatened with expulsion. The one time I told my leder that there was too much "poop" at groop ("How can you let So and So go on and on like that?") it got me, as they say, "in Dutch." I was a good student, though, so I only got probation.

Looking every which way but here

The aim of it all? I in the middle of AM.

Incomprehensibly, that aim came to be realized. However impossible it was to make it all how you wanted, and no matter what was happening, the lesson was always the same: Wake up (and smell the coughing). And I could work with that.

Best of all was—summer school in the Alps! We called it "camp." Sit-Chatters on retreat. Truly superb because of the guide and the altitude (you started at the top of a mountain and went up). But that's another "book."

Labor Intensive

From time to time, our branch of Sit-Chat hosted a weekend-long international conclave inviting leders from abroad to come together to compare notes (do, re, mi, and often fa). Some "visitoors" (as they were called) raised the level noticeably. I loved these events even though I was constantly up to my elbows in "hoot" water.

Were there guest lectures? Not really. There were classes: the leders and the "suppoort team." The leders would sit-chat and the suppoorters would wash the dishes, floors, towels, bedding, tabletops, toilets, and (occasionally) "feet" of the leders. The leders never washed a dish and the suppoorters never dissed a leder. There was lots of coffee, long hours, lumpy dorm mattresses on bunk planks (guess which class I was in)—but worth it; I needed to maintain constant efforts of attention lest I fall down on the floor in a "weepy heep."

Ed. Note: You bristle at what goes along with a hierarchy in spiritual organizations. But have you ever fawned over the person in charge, worthy or not? Could you see yourself doing that?

Similar week-long domestic intensives were called "werke periods," during which much was accomplished by the traditional means of "knitted broow." It was strenuous, sustaining attention during 18-hour days in a variety of uncomfortable and demanding conditions. All sorts of things were going on, including breaking down, acting up, and hiding out. Sometimes things got overly complicated. How many Sit-Chatters does it take to change a light bulb? At least five, on the "tool" team.

"Daaf, where do we need to make the change?"

"Ah. Give me a moment, Ibe, while I sketch out a map for us. Or would you rather we just all go there together and look at what's needed?" Moments later, at the joob site. "Murph-reinin, could you go get the new light bulb?"

"What wattage? Where are they stored?"

"Ah. Give me a moment, and I'll make you a list of the possible wattages and a map to the cabinet at the rear left of the third-floor hallway behind the bookcase. Or perhaps we should all go there together and look, to be sure we get the right kind."

Ten minutes later, back at the site. "Daaf, it's high up. Should we build a ladder? Is the switch off? How do I know when the current is on or off if the bulb is out?"

"Ah. Good questions, Ibe. Let me draw you a map to the circuit breaker box in the basement behind the washer. Jacob, draw out plans for a ladder. Make sure it will support 100 kilos and be stable on carpet and go up high enough. Murph-reinen, help him get the wood from the shed. Will we need anything from town?"

A morning of ladder-building. Then, the ascent.

"The old bulb is stuck in there. I don't want to force it. I don't want it to break off."

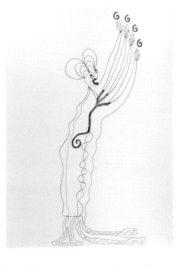

"Just come down, Ibe. We need to think some more about this. It's almost time for *collation*. Snool, gather up all the tools and Jacob's ladder, and put them away. We can sit and chat about the problem while we have our coffee."

Werke for werke's sake. Process rather than product. This approach was especially venerated at the annual event commemorating the birth of the Institoot's founder. Seriously elaborate preparations went on for days beforehand: it was all about being conscious while decorating the "room," creating exotic "food," and more. All done with great quietude and concentration. Then came the big night. The event itself. The celebration! Looking in, a passerby—out of ignorance—might comment, "Did someone die?"

Ed. Note: Poking fun at something you know well. It can be a problem, what happens in religious or spiritual organizations, because people, naturally, arrive at the house with their own baggage and unwittingly imitate the prevailing behavior form to fit in. On the other hand, practitioners at a spiritual center may feel that restraint and outer silence are an aid to concentration as well as a constant reminder, for oneself and others, why one has come.

The ideal in life, of course, is just being oneself and awake, with nothing artificial imposed. "Lord-and-Murphy," as you call it. By the way, underneath all you say, it seems to me, is deep gratitude for everything that happened.

Doctor of Philosophistry

Finally, I graduated. With highest honors, summa cum louty. My thesis, comparing several recent spiritual traditions, was entitled "Practice Makes Perfect—or Does It? In the Stream or Up the Creek?"

Some of my fellow graduates in the huvanities came up with the all-time best theses, expounding on the most obscure minutiae and having the longest titles ever:

"Investigating Local Hygiene Habits at Functionally Mismanaged Communal Retreats with Only Two Bathrooms"
Author: Ajax La Trine
Abstract: Why is the men's bathroom always more disgusting than the women's?

"Oh, Jools: Stress-Coping Strategies of Manna Lovers Confined at the Last Gulp Lookout"
Author: Nita Bach Remde
Abstract: Pre-adolescent behavior in sleep-deprived seekers on retreat getting their feathers plucked, including crying jags, hiding from authority figures, getting out of chores, smoking behind the shed, flirting, and sneaking into town.

"Group Survival Techniques of Suddenly Teacherless Practitioners Left to Their Own Devices: No Leopard, No Panther, Even the Ass Is Mammoth"
Author: Hoosen Charge
Abstract: Case studies from around the globe of what can happen when the warden dies and the inmates take over the asylum.

Lit?

"How to Make a Patchwork Quilt Kugel"
Author: Hal Acha
Abstract: Fusion cuisine at Christian Fundamentalist bar mitzvahs.

"The Sacral Advantage: Mitigating the Obstacles to Proper Construction of Meditation Cushions Designed for Long Periods of Minimally Effective Erect Sitting"
Author: Laura Buguper Ashley
Abstract: A behind-the-teams look at the overly

supervised construction, in silence, of one hundred hard, thick, round "sitting" cushions, accomplished by the sewing group at a ten-day retreat. Audio tape available.

"The Transparent Eyeball Gets Lasered: The Emersonian Challenge To Seeing in the Age of Just-Fix-Me-Quick"

Author: Weirs Ralph Waldo

Abstract: The blinding danger of instant solutions to self-esteem issues, such as becoming a disciple, or... becoming a guru!

"Platonic Conundrums: How Can We Reverse Deteriorating Conditions in Vulnerable Groups Without Alienating the Council Chieftain?"

Author: Phil Osfer King

Abstract: What do you do when your tribe is taken over by Chief Crazy Horse, or you are fed up with Sitting Bull?

"The Tragic Non-Use of Alliteration in the Poems of Mumi, Mitman, and Now Murphy"

Author: Rasa Loss

Abstract: The futility of restoring the poetic to poetry through language evoking powerful elevated states that are both unique to the speaker and universally unintelligible to those who listen.

"Only In Califor_ney Are There Teachers: Roto-Rooting the New Age Icons"
Author: Bunny Fluff, now a staff member, The Whole Irk Catalogue
Abstract: A compendium of the names of New Age practitioners and their specialties, including astral rejection, chakra juggling, rear coning, gonad magick, Akashic records management, and near-death sweat-lodge experiences.

"The Noethics of Big Gurus with Diamond-Studded Eyewear, Rolls Royces, and Mansions in Makealotakala"
Author: Venereal Bede
Abstract: A look beneath the golden robes of the spiritually well-endowed.

UPDATE: With great enjoyment I recently revisited my alma pater to discover the emergence of a new, lederless format called the "peer groop." Keep up the good werke, fellow lifelongers. We're on our way!

Ed. Note: Again, these citations are packed! Lots of additional material satirizing a variety of spiritual and cultural conditions, with an eye toward taking oneself a little more lightly?

CHAPTER 6

Head Case Studies

NEWS FLASH: The Federal Bureau of Identification has come up with a listening device that allows you to identify exactly what you're identified with. It even has a remote scanner so it works on nearby people, too. Think of it. You're driving down the road, remembering the wedding, and you can flip a switch to hear what every other driver at that instant is dreaming, too. Johnny Porsche, cutting you off while envisioning that Victoria's Secret model with the angel wings. Annabelle Blue Nova, on the way home from work, making lasagna in her head. Dr. Changelanes going down the mental list of Drugola's unfortunate side effects. Endless brains to surf. It's better than satellite radio!

Ever catalogue your thought-traffic? Mosquito mind, buzzing around on the windshield so you forget you're even in the car? It's mind's usual condition. Attention gone passive and mind very busy on the surface, pulled every which way. Here's what completely filled my rear-view mirror at moments this morning: internet out, no return call, last Tuesday, mold on strawberries, next Tuesday, what is

Who's pulling the strings?

that smell, confiscatory taxes, what is that noise, rude driver, rude fishwife at fish counter, rude clerk (it's an abrasive world). You know what I'm talking about.

Back up, Murph. (Whoa! Watch out for that Gremlin.) What exactly do you mean by "identification"? Because it's not your father's definition, "I identify with a certain group," meaning I am like them. And it's not "identify" meaning to label or classify. And it's not your driver's license.

Ed. Note: Good! Take time out from your usual rapid-fire delivery to define your key term. We need to catch our breath. "Identification" is not yet understood in this special context. Nor is the phrase "attention gone passive." But I think I understand what you mean. You're trying to show two different dispositions of mind:

(1) passivity and identification (mind busy coming up with answers; attention moving around all on its own, and hooked into whatever attracts it)

(2) awareness and stillness (mind quiet; attention not moving around but focused on impressions from senses and body now, and joining with this other Attention)

When one is identified, thoughts take over and there is no focusing on presence. In contrast, when one is awake, thoughts go by like clouds below, not disturbing one's focus. Inner quiet comes with tuning in to this other Attention. There may be moments with no thoughts, just impressions. Might one call this "non-identification"?

For those interested in awakening, the term "identification" is another word for (psychological) sleep. It's losing "I" while thinking about "X" or reacting to "Y." *Identification* is similar in meaning to the Buddhist term *attachment* in the sense that my mind and feelings glom onto something and I get lost in it. (Compare also the Tibetan Buddhist *sherpa*, meaning "taken up with baggage while trying to summit.")

If you hear someone say, "I can't get identified with it," that shows he understands how attention gets hooked so that the hook is then in charge. It's the peanut butter sandwich devouring me. It's harsh words that fester. It's the shopper in the narrow aisle nudging me with her cart so I want to slam her with mine. Beware. *The Thing Takes Over.* The fact that I can have a suddenly aggressive me-jerk reaction shows me my state—that I've been asleep, walking and talking in a dream, not aware I'm identified, a conduit for even more violence to come into the world.

When I'm unpleasantly identified, usually I know I'm in a tizzy. Does knowing break the spell? Possibly. Not always. I may try to reason my way through it or distract myself away from it. But there's momentum in stressing, wanting out of it, while automatic replay takes me back for more. If I persist in *seeing* myself, and the finer Attention appears, sanity returns. Whew! It certainly is humbling, though, what I'm like when hooked; it makes me feel for every human being suffering unconsciously in this world.

There are pleasant forms of identification, too, including those coming from an interest in higher consciousness. I'm still stuck on my own page but now it has marvelous new writing on it. "I am a seeker." "I am someone who is aware of finer energies." "I am a teacher." "I am one of the few who know what it's all about." Uh oh. *Neti, neti.* Not this, not that, say the Hindus, because I am not any thing thought, looked at, heard, felt, touched, tasted, smelled, excreted, said, read, believed, owned, or known. Maybe I'm the means by which such things are perceived—who knows? Who… lives? In any case, no matter how beautiful the writing, it's still adding to the page I assume I am.

And then, actual awakening: all of it lets go. *Tabula rasa* once more. Clean slate. Newborn pure awareness. A moment of transformation. Freedom.

Ed. Note: Do you mean "sherpa" or "shenpa"? (I'm guessing it's not a typo.) It's good that you've begun to talk about different forms of identification so one recognizes these things in oneself. Does one's "page" really go clear in the moments one is awake? It does feel as if the mind "unhooks" from things—even becomes "unhookable" for a while! Impressions come in but don't take one away.

The primary identification at the root of it all is that I'm this body, this thinker, this Murphy. But what are your examples of identification? Here's a recap of stories people told me when I asked.

Blindsided
Annie, 35, from Schenectady

Annie was at the ashram—wait, give it a chance—cleaning the floor of the meditation hall. Think Julia Roberts in *Eat, Bray, Love*. Naturally, Annie wanted to do well, be admired, and (as she put it) "pay for my keep!" People would be arriving any minute. She arranged the meditation cushions. She tried to raise the blinds on the one long window. When she pulled the cord, the blinds barely moved. Stuck. Drat! She tried again but couldn't get them to lift up, so she fiddled with the mechanism. Get help? But there was no time. Something in her said, "Just leave it," as she yanked the cord really hard. *Crash! Bang!* Guess what?

Just then, in walked everybody. Oh no! If only they would turn a blind eye. But there was nothing to be done. Annie had to sit down on her cushion for thirty minutes of meditation with the others. Did the sitting help? The blinds were on the floor behind her. All she told me was "I broke them, in my mind, over and over again."

DIAGNOSIS: *Identificationalis impatienzia inanimateobjectitus, Type A. With a flare-up of obsessivus thinkitus.*
PROGNOSIS: *Positive. If watched closely.*

Ed. Note: Yes, how many times have I yelled at a malfunctioning object as if it were intentionally messing up my day? Like Annie, one may be consumed by anything. Also, public exposure is especially painful because one wants to maintain one's image. There is the flavor of ownership in this kind of suffering: this is my stuff, and there's no way out, so leave me alone to suffer it until it runs out of steam. Ever felt that?

Sometimes one has to wait it out while being as self-aware as possible. Sometimes, though, it is precisely when one feels there is nothing one can do and no way *out that one becomes totally receptive to this other Attention. Nothing left for me but This. Was Annie able to experience that shift? To actually be related for a moment to the finer energy and know it? That alone would bring her freedom—a moment of what you mean by the word "transformation."*

Sink or Swim
Margaret, 64, from Fort Lauderdale

Sun red, just up over this ocean. Margaret looked out the window of her condo. No one in the pool. Time to swim laps, a daily meditation for her. She went early to have the pool all to herself. It was a cold day—wind kicking up white caps on the ocean. But the swimming pool was warm. They keep it at 104 for the seniors, bless 'em, who like to stand around and outdo each other's I-95 horror stories. But let her tell it:

"Down the steps. Into the water. Off I go. Weightless. Like flying. I push off from the wall. All of sudden, in the water over by the steps—a big hat with a head under it." (I hope it's attached to a body, or else this just took a gruesome turn.) "Someone in the pool. Suddenly, the Hat crosses right smack in front of me! Forcing me to stop." (Only one word for it: rude.) "I say nothing. Start again. But I have to keep looking up to see where she's walking in the pool. A few minutes later, the woman crosses in front of me—again! It feels intentional. Now I'm kicking too hard and too fast." (Foaming at the ankles.)

"No matter how I try to get back to some kind of quiet inside, this is not how I want it to be. So I get out of the pool. As I'm walking up the steps, she asks me how many laps I did. Like she wants to have a conversation. So I tell her that what she did was disturbing. And she says that I can't expect to have the whole pool to myself. Can you believe it? I know it should be nothing," Margaret admits to me, "but I thought about it all morning." (Even now, a little pissy.)

DIAGNOSIS: *Identificationalis imspecialurinmywaysho-vitis, with acute pain-body syndrome, a chronic condition that is dormant until it flares up under stress.*
WARNING: *Highly contagious.*
PROGNOSIS: *Positive. Subject is self-aware enough to manage the condition.*

Ed. Note: You use the term "self-aware." Is that different from being awake? With self-awareness, one thinks; with waking up, one sees. If Margaret is below "see" level, she would need to wake up—difficult in turbulent waters—in order for the hold on her to be broken. And I think you're right: she gets identified again just telling the story. But sometimes one needs to suffer one's behaviors until one gets a taste of how they repeat and repeat until the appropriate response appears: attention truly mobilizing. But how to tell a drowning man, here, take another gulp?

Judge Much?
James, 35, from California

At a retreat luncheon, the teacher posed a question. "Who here thinks they have a reliable mind?"

The four people most lost in thought raised their hands.

James wasn't about to volunteer for whatever was coming. He'd been hauling rocks in a wheelbarrow all morning and just wanted to take a nap. A topic was introduced. People opined about it.

One said, "My mind is reliable only when yak yak yak…."

James was staring at a knot in the floor, thinking, *Are you kidding?*

"The awakened mind is oompha oompha oompha…."

You don't know what you're talking about. You're totally asleep.

"I read in Leibniz that gobble gobble gobble…."

These intellectuals. Thinking won't ever get it.

Then, suddenly—startling—as from a great distance—

He heard his name called. "James?"

Huh?

DIAGNOSIS: *Identificationalis judgmentalostfocusitis*
PROGNOSIS: *Positive. Flare-ups will not be a problem. Subject gets it.*

Ed. Note: Your James realizes that he's been sitting there judging while sitting there thinking he's awake. If one could notice this all the time, one could wake up! Fortunately, life presents constant challenges that help one observe how one is. What is it like to hear a person without the filter of judgment, so focused in Attention that one can just let him be? Any experience with that?

If You Know What's Good For You
Jenny, 22, from Westport

"Single-use plastic bags are a big threat to the environment," said the guest speaker at Jenny's environmental studies class at an elite liberal arse college. Afterwards, on her iPhone in the limo, receiving an invitation to lead a local ban-the-bag campaign, Jenny responded, "Woot!" (She's majoring in Netiquette.)

The next day, after yoga, Jenny bagged her first supermarket manager. He agreed to a trial run. Victory! No more plastic bags. They kept a few paper ones under the counter, but you had to ask for them (like condoms, in the olden days).

A week later, as she stood on line at the checkout counter, she "felt great watching people with my reusable bags." She was taking notes for an article (tentatively entitled "Going Green, My New Bag," or possibly "Today's Green Grocer: It's In the Bag," or how about "The Old Bag Gets Dumped").

Ahead of her at the register was, as Jenny put it, "an elderly gentleman, about 60." The man asked for a paper bag.

The checkout girl stopped texting and pulled one from under the counter (thinking, "Alta cocker"). "Why don't you use the new ones," she grumbled. (Rude. What's happened to customer service, by the way? Don't they "train" anymore?)

Jenny watched as the man held up a package of raw chicken. Despite its thin plastic wrapping, it left some ruddy liquid on the counter. "Not sanitary," he said. "Salmonella. This package leaks. I have to wash your bags in hot water and then dry them in the dryer. Takes energy, takes detergent. What's it even made of—this cheap fiber stuff—probably toxic, from China." (Yup. Flame retardant. Asbestos in there for sure. Arsenic too, maybe. To kill the germs.) "Can you even sanitize it?"

Jenny looked the other way, feigning interest in the magazine rack. She admitted to me, "I felt like I'd bullied him. Like I hadn't thought it through." The moment she got back in the limo, though, she Googled for more information.

DIAGNOSIS: *Identificationalis youthfulhormonalzealotiosis, with incipient ownershititis.*
WARNING: *Ownershititis is dangerous, often intractable, when subject is older.*
PROGNOSIS: *Positive. Cure is probable with advanced yoga.*

LORD HAVE MURPHY

Ed. Note: Jenny personifies youthful exuberance identified with a cause. She is well-meaning and, like her, one wants to be a good steward of our planet. Identification with anything, though, can make one myopic. (In the future, Jenny may need to beware of being taken advantage of by people with high-sounding causes masking hidden or short-sighted agendas.)

These stories illustrate some of the common forms of identification: becoming entirely occupied with an object, a feeling, a reaction, a judgment, a cause. Driven by ego, belief, substances, habit. Interacting with others unconsciously.

Do you know this quote from Emerson? "Things are in the saddle and ride man."

Publish or Punish
Murphy, from New York
(Rejection Letter 3)

Dear Mr. Murphy:

We read with interest page one of your work of "interdimensional humor" entitled *Lord Have Murphy*. Unfortunately, your book is not a good fit for our list, so we are not interested in publishing it now or ever.

Your premise is interesting. However, your authorial voice has a kind of irreverent reverence that will confuse the average reader.

Of course, another publishing house might not have a completely different response to your work.

Understandably, as good businessmen, we are interested only in books that will sell. You have no platform. We wish you success with your project.

Sincerely yours,

Mack E. Avelly

Executive Assistant to the
Assistant Executive Editor
HARPOONCULLEM, San Francisco

LORD HAVE MURPHY

(Rejection Letter 143)

Dear Mr. Murphy:

Seriously?

Best wishes,
Gitch Manitou
LITTLE PRESS ON THE PRAIRIE

Me in all my glory

Arrrggggh! Excuse me while I pull the knife out of my heart.

And here I thought— as I sit in it now—that my shit doesn't stink. That my plumage is beautiful.

Guess not. But I can work with… I can… sniffle, sniff…. Oh well. If at first you don't succeed, try, try epub.

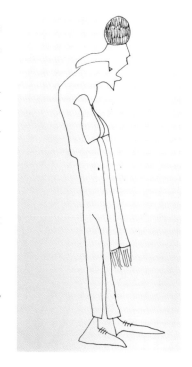

Ed. Note: "Interdimensional" humor—meaning it's there but we can't see it?

Perhaps say a bit more about "as I sit in it now." When a reaction is triggered, how do you bear your own behavior to wake up?

Also, you may be giving the impression that identification is a bad thing. Is it? Does the shock of realizing one's been asleep turn one toward waking?

The only problem with identification is getting identified with it—thinking it's a problem. It's just life in the passing lane. If there's the aroma of minestrone in the hall, of course my mind becomes a bowl of soup. If someone ruffles my feathers, of

Attention that can stay

course it's pluck you. Golden opportunity here! To sit in my own stuff—really notice how I am—and wake up, thank you. *See* without interfering. The way I deal with identification is to try to become aware of my body, objectively and impartially, while the event is happening. Yes, it takes practice. Not to change things but to *see*.

I can't approach an identification with the intention of manipulating it or covering it up because that diverts me to yet another side alley in which I don't *see*. Lost in worry? Jumping for joy? Daydreaming at the sink? Raging inside? But noticing that's where you're at? Here's your chance!

All these self-styled gurus who say that I can stop suffering by altering my thinking—big misunderstanding. Robs me of the possibility of *seeing* and opening to a higher level of consciousness. For me it's not about stopping thoughts when they're negative, and it's not about stopping feelings when my ego gets pricked. It's about finding the consciousness that embraces all of it, limited by none of it. Life in the merge lane.

It doesn't matter how long my list of daily IDs or what's on my page. The attention, when passive, simply gets occupied elsewhere; it happens; so whatever reminds me to activate attention and come home is awesome. Going away and coming back. All one. All part of the same process of waking up. Transitory blips lose their glue when Lord is found here, too.

Lord-and-Murphy. Attention that can stay.

Ed. Note: I'm glad you recognize that identification is a help—even a big help—the necessary reminder of one's state. There is that jolt when one realizes that, despite one's intention to be present, one drifted away or is in the grips of something. One may react and complain about it—yet What is animating even that commentary? The question prompts a look. Interest shifts. Seeing oneself calls back one's attention and restores awareness.

Usual mind and seeing: one needs both for waking up. It's an important point that you make. Also, aside from common sense and common decency—not so common these days—what is the safeguard against unconscious behavior that harms? When Attention is the focus, impressions do not take one away into identification; on the contrary, they are received consciously and bring one back to oneself.

CHAPTER 7

Maximizing the Art of Living

People who reckon they know everything
are a great irritation to those of us who do.

—Gnothi Seauton

I arose this morning with a thirst. To nurse at the breast of MyOther Nature, the one that is (not mine and) hidden from my usual mind. Sometimes I leave myself post-it reminders lest I lose the day in sleep. When I went to the fridge, there was a note on it, to help me write: *"First learn the meaning of what you say, and then speak."* Good advice from Epictetus, grandfather of the original self-help manual indicating the route to inner peace. And reading him again got me thinking: is what you offer the milk of transformation, O Epicteatus? Or more a case (carton) of Epicteaseus? Close, but not the real thing. Soy milk, maybe. But without the *Soy*.

It's human nature to want to share with others what helps in this life. The hitch comes when self-help instruction poses as a path to awakening. So let me, humbly, correct an erroneous notion. A new way of thinking is not the same as waking up. Another manner of behaving is not the same as waking up. Being awake in this shower of energy is completely different. At any moment, you're aware you're in it or you're not.

WARNING: READ NO FURTHER if you enjoy the self-enhancement buffet and already

understand that it has little to do with waking up. Just skip this chapter. I don't want to spoil your delight in a tasty favorite.

But wait! Are you sure you get the difference? Because there appears to be a blurring of the line between self-help and awakening. Can you behave your way into waking up? What are some of our spiritual-life coaches offering?

Ed. Note: I agree that there is misunderstanding in this area. You make a crucial distinction between thinking and waking. Analyzing oneself in terms of some new information, behaving like one believes a saint would, or cultivating positive thoughts may be part of a learning process, but all take place in sleep. Waking up is a different level. I hope you can illustrate how this is so. One needs to know in oneself the difference between ordinary and higher consciousness.

Everything in Self-Help but The Self?

The necessity for "payment" has long been part of many true teachings: in order to receive, one pays to the Higher, with effort, with attention. The problem comes when gurus say *payment* but mean *pay them*.

And pay for what, exactly? Is awakening a desirable add-on to self that can be acquired and possessed? A Now Age version of the ever-marketable "get-in-touch-with-God-to-get-a-leg-up-on-others"?

Let's sample the data. Here are recent examples of approaches to "higher consciousness" culled from magazines, supermarket flyers, and best sellers. Which ones are about waking up?

1. At a European training facility for meditative levitators, eyewitnesses testify that initiates, after paying a first-class fare, "fly around the room." (Too literal a take? "Higher" = "up on the ceiling"?)

2. More than one traveling teacher offers soulful seminars and online courses—each with its own special terminology and testimonials—plus an Impressive-Name "World Center." (It's located in the Cloud. If only it were the Cloud of Unknowing!) A sample from this year's online top-award winner: *"Your Real Self™ is happiness whereas your Individual Self™ is joy. Your Prickly Self™ blocks both when you resist what happens in your life."*

3. In an ambitious resort in the desert, a self-described "New Age Self-Help Guru" charges $9000

Too much information

($10,000 for get-into-the Club Level) to train you in the not so secret skill of energy attraction. Will positive thinking turn you into a "spirit warrior" *plus* help you sell more widgets?

4. In the name of spreading Zen Buddhism, a kung fu master in China welcomes many more Hollywood movies as a way, in his words, of "branding Shaolin worldwide."

5. A local lightworker advertises "initiation so transformative" that in only two sessions the God energy in you will uplift you to a plane (an Airbus heading for Bora Bora, I hope) from which you can heal others. (Hmm. Possibly. The power of suggestion is huge. Higher energies do heal. And in just two sessions, eh?)

6. Across town another practitioner invites you to stand with one foot in a bucket of hot water, the other in a bucket of cold, while your right hand karate-chops point 9 at the top of your skull. (Dunno. Sounds very Zen. Might work.)

Ed. Note: Is this for real? I like to think you're exaggerating for effect—but I'm not sure. You're alerting us to what awakening is not (special powers, mind control, suggestibility, the placebo effect, self-trance, group trance, all-in-the-head pep talks, money-driven psychobabble).

I hope you will also give us the (as it were) other side of the coin and look at what form of payment or effort is actually needed to wake up.

Shifty Business

One mega-best-selling pataphysician, well-versed in East-West lingo and well-loved for such enriching tips as *"Give, in order to get,"* sort of assumes that waking up is something *I get*. He makes a case for—and is living proof of—this business of using spirituality to solve my every problem and create for myself boundle$$ succe$$. Deep pockets? Show me!

"Let us understand that spiritual analysis of one's position is the process by which a troubled investment yields windfall profits. By identifying the impact cost of your

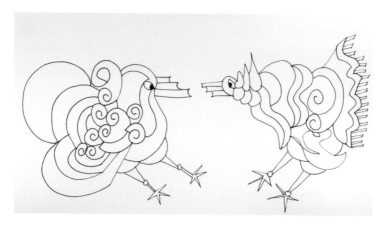

Let me tell you how it is

feelings about a problem, you can do a swap in real time to a return-to-maturity interpretation, shifting from your risky contracted level of consciousness to pure profitability in the field office of limitless being. Trading in the wrong currency? Simply analyze your net effective income in the moment, and if there's noise, opt for the no-load fund of expanded awareness, and then incorporate it into your consciousness portfolio."

Got that? As transparent as a hedgefund-hog in a swamp at midnight. What's the bottom (feeder) line?

"To sum up, when faced with a threat to your net worth, examine what in you is a negative carry, and do a non-parallel shift to improve your yield curve."

Except, who has ever shifted into a *higher* level of consciousness by analyzing anything? Waking up is not something that happens through applying concepts. On the contrary, the only role the conceptual mind needs to play is to exit the building.

Another slippy-slope:

If by chance there actually *is* a shift to a higher level, and I try to *use* a moment of waking up for a purpose other than continuing to wake up in this moment—like, say, to show off, slim down, or cash in—Poof! It's finished. Thread cut. Down I go. Although no one who is asleep, including me, may notice. The Self, apparently, is Self-protected.

As it happens, indeed there *is* a spiritual solution to every difficulty: the elixir of wakefulness permeates the sap that's identified. That's how you hit pay dirt. (Murphy, this is a negative carry. Quick! You need a Shower.)

Lighten up, Murph. Jealous much? How many best sellers have you written? You're as militant as a fundie saving souls at a skeptics rally. Besides, one man's stinkweed may be another man's dungwort. And it's frivolous to focus on some bit of commercialism, considering the atrocities done to people every day in this world.

At odds with myself

In the face of such terrors, though, maybe our hope for real change is that enough human beings actually wake up. Just enough so a finer energy begins circulating among us. Just enough to permeate the atmosphere. Consciousness can be catching. To make a difference, it may not even have to go viral.

Ed. Note: You take a strong position: that every person wanting to wake up is urgently needed, so do not mislead anyone. About being misled, sometimes one has to go down a side alley to discover for oneself if it's a dead-end.

Let it be. Trust that those who are waking up will not be misled for long. The milk of human fineness may not yet be everyone's cup of tea. Epictetus would call this finger-wagging a sign that you, Murph, have made no "moral progress" because you are going against what you know deep down: that we cannot help what we do in sleep.

A Bit More on Tranceformation

Or can we? What if a little taste of attention is a dangerous thing? What if these innerstructors have had just enough transcendent experiences to take us to new hypes and put us on a primrose path full of excitement that will only wane, leading to a dire end? For example, consider another recent offering from one of the World's 50 Most Quantifiable Spiritual Teachers. This well-intended mentor's thousandth book from Make Hay House is called *90 Days to Supreme Inner Peace and Cashcading Wealth*. It's based on the rehab-tested theory that it takes 90 days to establish a new habit.

From the introduction:

"I am fortunate to feel God, Brahma, Jesus, Buddha, Lao Tzu, Pele, Saint Augustine, Shiva, Mohammed, the Pope, my fans, the Favored Ones, and Spirit informing every step I take. And I warranty that you, too, can move up to your highest self, and appreciate all the wondrous things that arrive daily in your life, and have everything your heart desires, so long as you can make yourself feel it is already yours.

"Let's begin with my modern version of the life-altaring Yoga Sutures *that came to me in a rainforest during my year-long study of Patandjolly:* 'LET GO OF GRUMPY. LET GO OF DOPEY. LET GO OF SLEEPY.'"

Ah, yes. Pithy. Bringing me all the inner peace of a caged dodo bird.

Promise much? And are we taking just a little too much OWNERSHIP of our life, here? Just a tad narcissistic? (From the Greek "narkissos," meaning "kiss of sleep.") I'm hungry for this, but am I being suckered? *"Live by your sun, without regulations, without resistance, accepting all, humbly, in unity, calmly, effortlessly, in the current."* But who here can truly *do* these things you

The Yoga Sutures of Patandjolly

suggest? No matter how many times I gaze at the maxims on your perpetual-wisdom flip calendars, enlightened note cards, and inner-peace candles, I would have to be living in Attention to live in Attention. Behavior modification cannot bring a higher state.

Lord knows, I need encouragement on the journey. And you make it sound so easy. But neither self-analysis nor cognitive behavior therapy changes my level. I may try to deal with an unpleasant situation as you suggest, with a new way of thinking about it, even a different behavior. And then I'll believe—even sadder—that this kind of "doing" actually puts me in the Tao's flow. But mimicking the attributes of waking up is not waking up. So I'm doomed to fail. Maybe even worse off now. The disappointed rubber band snapping back after a dream of having stretched.

What exactly is the pithfall here?

Reinforcing the dream that by thinking differently I will be different, that thinking is the kind of payment, the proper coin, that brings awakening. That if I manipulate my behavior, my state will change. Or at least my city. I'll get out of Needmore and move up to Eureka or maybe Niceville, where I'll have an easier time of it. Still in the same old country of Slumberland, though. A temporarily-improved Murphy, a temporarily-happier Murphy, a temporarily-fixed Murphy—but not an awake Murphy. Maybe one day I'll be able to change my socks just by thinking "Argyle."

Ed. Note: One truth, and many paths to it, all of which take one into the Unknown. You are saying that what the pseudo-gurus advise is not one of them. Do you know this quote from the Tao Te Ching? "A path that is a path already traced is not the Path." Or this, from The Yoga Sutras of Patanjali, "For those who have an intense urge for Spirit and wisdom, it sits nearby, waiting." This other Attention, always there when recognized.

Most teachers genuinely want to help, and there are wonderful practitioners today in many spiritual disciplines. We are awakening. But you are speaking of someone knowingly (ignorantly?) manipulating others while claiming to bring higher consciousness. To you, it's worse than muddying the waters. It's a violation of the sacred. So it's good to speak up. There are dangers here for people. More than wounded pride at one's gullibility or dollars and time lost. I'm thinking of the ones who died in a faulty sweat lodge because they blindly trusted the "criminal" leading them in there.

If the instructor is charismatic, enjoys a position of authority, or appears successful, one's own suggestibility may be difficult to see. How to distrust what influences one in sleep?

Row, Row, Row Your Boat

As long as we're paddling down this river, might as well put in another oar. Still very popular in the literature is the Leaky Boat School of Self-Perfecting. The idea is that I'm leaking energy all the time through the expression of negative emotions so I have no energy to wake up. This approach was all the rage last century. My white load comes out yellow—that person took my parking space—look how he spoke to me—the bureaucrats are in my face—I dropped my iPhone on the marble floor—(Idiot!) All day long, leak, leak, freak. A scarcity mentality: not enough "force" left in me to awaken. I must stop the leak in order to wake up. Really?

I think the popularity of this leaky idea stems

from being ashamed (rightfully so) of how I act some-times, so I should control my nasty outbursts; I have been told—and want—to do no harm. Or maybe the idea of "not expressing negative emotions" was given as an inner exercise to provide frequent reminders to wake up—but the waking-up part got lost. Sure, I'd like to be a universally calm-nice person, like the big boys. But I'd rather be awake. It's when I'm in the stream of Attention that I feel actual kindness flow through to you. And how do I know I cannot wake up in a heated moment? And why not the same treatment for positive emotions? I'm just as asleep in them, too.

When my interest is sidetracked from awaken-ing to manipulating my behavior, a possible moment of relation with the finer energy is lost—plus, I may think that what I'm doing is waking up. My first time at the Sit-Chat-Ananda Institoot in Amsterdam even I may have said to myself, "Ah, Murph-reinin, you are annoyed right now, but look how you are able to control the expression of your emotions. You're werking now." It was very easy to become very busy with pretending to be collected. In Holland we call this "going down the toobs."

By the way, the term "non-expression" is not quite accurate. By the time we notice it, the emotion is already "expressed"—isn't it?—in the pit of the stomach, the set of the mouth. Who is quick enough to stop cortisol, once triggered, from expressing itself in the bloodstream?

Maybe stressful events become the necessary karate-chop to the head so I remember I *can* wake up. And waking up cannot mean swallowing negativity so I ulcerate my gut. To me it means *seeing* all in its full glory. Calling back my attention and discovering afresh this other Attention—that neither needs energy nor takes energy, that is always there in abundance in me, whether I'm pouting or praying. I don't have to behave a certain way to wake up!

Murph, do you understand? This is your practice. And you love it. It doesn't matter how you are or how long it takes—it's a new way to live. *Seeing* is freeing. It's thrilling to discover that even now, even when grumping around, just look—and is it there, the light? Brightening wide, now that you notice and keep noticing, as you move into the next moment?

Any breath. Just as I am. In the glow.

I suppose someone could say that when I fall back asleep it's because my attention has leaked out and is lost—but that's not accurate either. It hasn't leaked: it's simply occupied elsewhere. On the playground swings when the teacher summons. Instantly it can be called back.

Merrily, Merrily, Merrily, Merrily

Each time the sun comes out, none of these dust-ups is of concern. I am not a problem. You are not a problem. *Life is but a dream* from which we awaken.

Murph, *take heart*. Trust the process working us. Feel its power. So very near—right now! Stay exactly as you are—*see* how it is in abdomen, jaw, face, breath, hands, toes—the light around you—all at once. Not changing a thing. Not necessary when attention mobilizes. What if the treasure lies not in the details but in the *seeing*?

Now, I remember. Now I begin to come alive.

Everything in life can help me wake. Blessed life teaches at every turn. Cocky? Just wait a second; something will come along to show me where I'm really at. Leaky? There is a force in me that cannot leak. Disillusioned? Part of the process. I need to separate the gold from the cash. But I can work with that.

To each his own. Self-help has its role, too. Sometimes we just need relief. Sometimes we just need to read that book on happiness. We're hurtin' here. We've been hammered about happiness for so long—others have it, must get it, or get it back! Re-grooving, attitude adjustment, inspirational books, body work, prayer, laughter, healing modalities, energy medicine, visualization, positive thinking, right eating, all give us strength to go on for another half day. Any time we can, we try to treat one another with kindness. I don't know the path that each of us is on, or the timing, or the way things are meant to unfold. What I do know is what I wish for us all: awakening.

Ed. Note: It's striking that once you turn your attention

to waking up you cheer up. It no longer matters, your reactions or what prompted them. All of it recedes in importance when you become related again to the finer energy. A new feeling arises, a love of being conscious, and in that, the wish to continue living this new way. And the well-wishing for all is genuine.

Maybe it's just the self-helpers' language that's my problem. Words like "transforms" and "conscious," that once promised something spiritual, now describe, respectively, a new shampoo and a clothing line. That's why there's that smell. Oh well. Just men and women doing their worldly thing; nobody special, Murph, just like you. What, you were

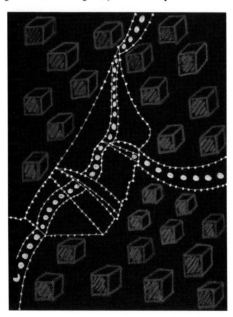

Seeing my way through

expecting Jesus maybe?

All we need is to redefine a few key terms so we all know what we're talking about.

Glossary of Popular Self-Help Terms

TRANSFORMATION. Transitory information about how to cope as a cheerier me.

INNER PEACE. When the inner din eases due to a piece of advice.

INTENTION. Holding oneself "in tension" to prevent resumption of bad habits.

HIGHER SELF. (1) The one halfway up the ladder; (2) myself on medical marijuana.

HIGHEST SELF. (1) The one at the top of the ladder; (2) myself on LSD.

MEDITATION. While sitting quietly, me editing out the narration in my head.

CONSCIENCE. The science of conning others into believing anyoldthing.

No harm, no foul. Happier people—even for a weekend—are better than murderers. So, cheerleaders on this field of dreams, cheer us on. Obviously, our team loves to listen.

Ed. Note: One feels the lash of love here—that you care that people not dupe or be duped. But it must be very seductive to be wildly successful producing works on "higher" consciousness even though that may not be what's presented. Perhaps even near-teachings have their place. Ultimately, one may need to experience different things to discover a truth felt in oneself.

Please, Curb Your Dogma

They're everywhere—aren't they?—these terse quips for living. Self-help in short form. Apt maxims to help us through the day. Smart tweets. Sound bites. Wisdom in a one-liner. With a smiley face. Laughter is freeing!

On a car bumper: *Honk if you love silence.*

Outside a church: *Less Facebook, more Good Book.*

On my refrigerator magnet: *Don't worry. Be happy.* Profound words. Except… was I absent that day in school when we all learned how to stop worrying so we never fret again? Yet this sunny sentiment can change my outlook for an hour. 'Fess up, Murph. You're a self-helper from way back. You may have *been* Epictetus (more likely, Xantippe). You love those fingers pointing at the moon. You're a moon-pointer yourself! So, if I may, what is your main point?

Attention Is the Teacher

In the maze of sages, how to *see* my way through? Because a list of credentials doesn't guarantee a person is awake. What happens in me as I listen to that person? What is the litmust test?

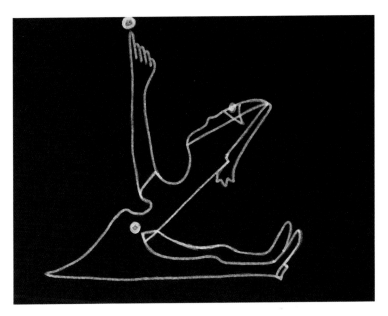

The main point

Focused attention, my compass. As present as possible, actively alert, as often as possible. Sensing my body, so attention can stay. Aware of breathing. Listening. A teacher may appear when I'm ready, when there is an abiding interest in waking up. At least that's been the case with me.

How do I know if the teacher is genuine?

The teacher's eyes upon me may steady me in wakefulness. Or the face looking at me becomes a mirror in which I recognize exactly how it is with me in this instant. My level of consciousness goes up, attention is activated, I am entirely different from a moment ago, and I know it.

Down the road, the time comes when the "outer" teacher is no longer needed. When Self helps. A spiritual guide is one in whose presence I come to discover the Teacher in me: the finer Attention. Returning to it restores peace in myself.

Ed. Note: When one is alert in the presence of a true guide, one may feel the non-ordinary atmosphere of Attention. One may feel the love that wishes only one's awakening, nothing else. One may feel supported in sustained attention. The more one becomes aware of the finer energy, the more one can become aware of the finer energy.

In these last paragraphs, you are straightforward. Readers may not be used to it! But risk it. We have laughed with you in the face of our foibles; here you tell the reader there is hope in finding the true teacher. Explore where this voice takes you. For balance, what about writing some positive stories showing moments of non-identification, of individuals waking up?

CHAPTER 8

Wakebook

Have you heard about the great opens-the-Source software now available called Wakebook? You have to wake up to get past your own page.

It's all about streaming live video of yourself. It's reality-show you! Try it. Camera on. *Click.* Feel that camera on you? Your body being seen—posture, facial expression—as you read these words? That's live video while it's happening. I'm actually streaming right now.

Ed. Note: It seems like you're saying that a first step in waking up is to stay exactly as you are—change nothing—and simply feel yourself under observation whatever you're doing. How do you get the "camera" to stay on or turn on often?

When I've stopped streaming but don't realize it, the app pings to remind me. Sometimes I don't hear the ping. But when I do, this shifting of attention to Observing Mode may bring on Receiving Mode. That's the exciting part. *Seeing* me-like-this *while* me-is-like-this—observing rather than running away—

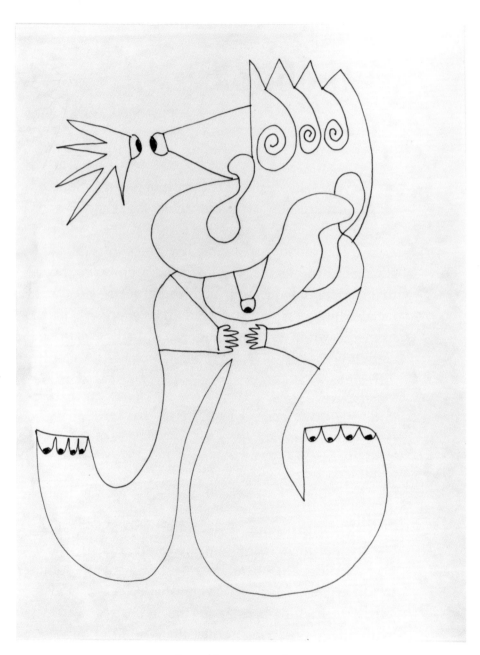

Something sees me here

allows the finer energy to appear; and if it does, then who cares anymore what the "me-like-this" is. It's history! Something much more compelling is now on the scene.

And that's how you get past your own page.

What exactly takes place? It's a mystery. Here's my over-simplified theory (I didn't write the app): somehow mind-here-observing connects with body-here-seen and feelings-here-interested-in-seeing; all three coming together permits perception of what's animating the whole.

The earlier version of the app used to crash because it was about feelings only. The necessity of bringing together the three parts was not understood. The old version involved taking a snapshot of yourself in a moment of negativity. You'd "pin it" instead of "stream it." You'd take every painful thing you didn't like about yourself and "pin it" to your page (it's Painterest!). When the accruing items reached the tipping point—*Help! I can't stand me anymore*—you'd pray and hit DELETE.

(What you get now, if you try that, is an ERROR message.)

Ed. Note: It's good that you present the special meaning of "seeing" and how it brings about unity of mind, body, and feelings for a moment of waking up. It's good what you say about observing, too, that it needs to be active and neutral for one's level to go up. Otherwise one is living in only one part of oneself, sidetracked by a thought or feeling (such as not liking something or trying to get rid of it). But there is an Intelligence in oneself that bypasses thoughts. If I understand what you say, "seeing" can access that.

What kinds of videos get streamed? Jolly Murphy, tired Murphy, snobby Murphy, worried Murphy, snacking Murphy, yacking Murphy, nervous Murphy, angry Murphy, kind Murphy, reading Murphy, washing-hands Murphy. Brushing-teeth Murphy. Superstitious Murphy is fun, this believer in wacky things. Like God had something to do with the outcome of my last dental appointment. If that hadn't happened, then this might have happened, and then that would have been a big problem. Because it's all about me.

What else do I believe?

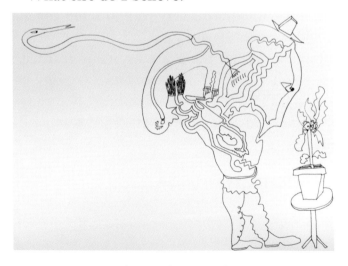

The ever-busy mind

What I Often Believe

—That I am my body, its physical condition, my thoughts, my feelings, my story

—That all the random events that happen to me are significant because, well, they happen to *me*

—That I walk around as inflated as a hot air balloon but rarely notice until I get pricked

—That I must control things as much as possible so they go smoothly

—That beliefs run my life, influencing what I think, say, and do

Hmm. So few beliefs. There must be more. May I have a peek at your list? Thank you. Ah, yes. More mind-made manacles. The ones under the nadir. Medulla oblongotcha. Beliefs (the Big Addiction) often involve ownership (the Big Trap). Everything is mine. Particularly tricky in the spiritual arena.

I May Still Believe

—That my experiences and understanding of higher states belong to me (The-One-Who-Thinks-He-Glows)

—That certain people have cornered the market on higher states, and I have no chance of waking up without learning from them (The-Ones-Who-Seem-To-Own)

How to get past your "own" page?

Ed. Note: Ownership. You brought up the topic in your parody of spiritual blogging. It's worth bringing up again because so much of life is limited by the belief that one is a somebody who owns things (my body, my thoughts, my accomplishments, my interests, my dog, my stuff). One does not have to give up anything, though, to free oneself. (One can get just as identified with giving up something as with owning it, yes?)

Have you heard the phrase, "To awake, to die, to be reborn"? Perhaps it's not a sequence in time but an instantaneous shift: to discover again the finer energy in oneself, to die to the identified part that dominates or thinks it owns, to be reborn into higher consciousness in this moment. Every time one wakes up.

A reboot may be necessary if there is longtime involvement with "my thing"—a set of ideas, an organization, even an approach to waking up. Loving the process is one thing; forging an identity out of it is another. Too invested? No joy in Mudville? Time to reboot. During grad school, I rebooted (unplugged for a while, then reconnected). Everything that takes place is necessary, I guess, because "we're here in lesson" (belief number 1212)… AND… it's happening to *me*. Oops. There again. Up against it.

Or, AM I?

Ping!

Streaming now….

And I see….

That this body is a marvel—but not the whole story.

Ah! Now I remember how the new app works. It's not about getting rid of anything. Forget the DELETE key. It's the *seeing* that matters! Because it calls my attention, all parts come together, and something fine can permeate.

Ping!

OPTION. SHIFT.

Streaming now….

RETURN…

…to this other Attention, unlimited, unknown. To let the rest go for a moment and…

ENTER.

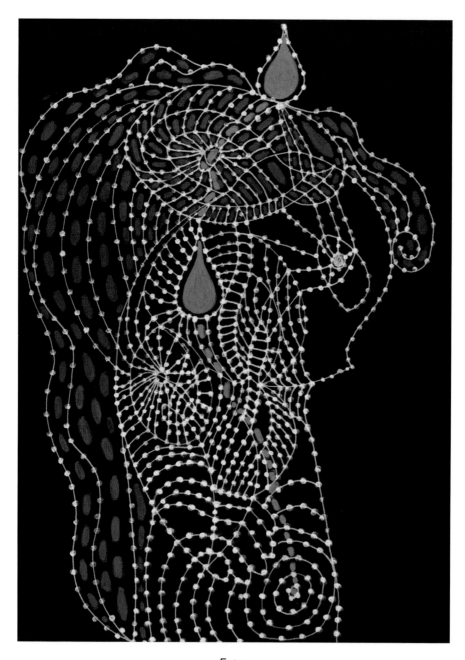

Enter

CHAPTER 9

Picture This

In the moments we embody the finer energy, the Goodness of it flows through us into the world. Many times during the day, non-identification becomes possible. It's already happening in our lives. I know this from phone interviews. When I called, everyone had a story to tell. I listened attentively. Oh, maybe once or twice I held the phone away from my ear for, say, a minute or two—like you do sometimes when your brother calls—but I recorded it all. So here's a recap, including some first-hand accounts. Are these stories of non-identification? Lord knows. They are little epiphanies. Glimmers of awakening.

Ed. Note: I'm very glad you're giving us stories of non-identification, too. I hope you include some of your own in the mix.

Music of the Spheres
Annie, 35, from Schenectady

An evening of music was planned at the ashram. Who would coordinate it? Annie volunteered, God (and everyone else) love her. What she really wanted was to be part of the chorus, but a long time ago her second grade teacher—I'll spare you the blow-by-blow—embarrassed her in front of the class making it clear that Annie couldn't carry a tune (ouch!). Poor Annie. Still carrying that tune. Anyway, at rehearsals, she made sure everyone had the right sheet music, the piano was tuned, and the floor was clean.

"We don't have enough altos," the director told her one morning.

"I'm an alto," said Annie.

So she joined the chorus and learned to sing the alto parts. Or pretended to sing. Those unsure eyes darting around to the others. That straining to hear the elusive strand of notes in the four-part harmony. The timid singing very very softly. Truth? She probably mouthed the words. But there were only a few altos, her voice was needed, so the director worked with her privately.

Performance day arrived. Dress rehearsal tanked. It made her as twitchy as a squirrel in a dog park. There was this one place where the altos had to come in, after a pause, on exactly the right note. No matter how many times the director went over it, no luck. Finally, he motioned to stop, and said, "One of the women is singing bass with the men." Annie's cheeks flushed. She tried to listen better. The pianist played the altos' line twice. Would Annie ever get it?

At dinner that evening in the large hall, she

couldn't eat. Her stomach was a knot-now-thank-you. Picture her: heart racing as she unfolded that well-worn piece of sheet music and stared at it for the zillionth time. That one note. Where the whole thing, as she put it, "fell to ruin."

Meal over. Dishes cleared. The big moment. Annie took her place with the others in front of everyone and their teacher. This is the interesting part. She said she could feel her teacher's eyes on her—she made a big point of that. Maybe he helped her. Just sayin'.

The director grinned at the singers, no doubt with an irresistible glint in his eye. Smile, everybody; no one but Greek tragedians like a grim chorus.

The piano began to play. With those first notes, everything changed for Annie. But let her tell it:

"The harmonies were so beautiful! I felt like I was singing in a celestial choir. I was able to listen to the others and blend with them. We came in on that note perfectly. It was all so natural, and bright, and free. I was so happy to be there, with the others, grateful, just to be singing, in front of our teacher. The room glowed. My face was beaming—"

How she could sing out, the One in her that is full of joy!

Ed. Note: I remember Annie, the woman who broke the blinds. Here again she seems unsure of herself, wanting to do well, wanting to feel like one of the group. And then, when she sings in front of her teacher, Annie crosses the threshold for a moment. Out of her usual mindset. Vibrating higher. In the Unity with others. Belonging to something much more than just the singing group.

Getting Whacked
James, 35, from California

James, a stand-up guy, told me what happened after lunch that day at the retreat when his name was called. He didn't get to rest. He was assigned to paint the cabinet near the piano in the main hall before a recital. James likes painting, paying attention to each stroke as the paint glides on. He had just about finished when he noticed he needed to do the trim way at the top. It would take only a minute. Go all the way back to the workshop for a step stool? Nah. He grabbed the piano bench and stepped up on it. Crack!

Panic! This is where it gets good. No one around. He quickly jimmy-rigged the broken leg, put the splinters back so it looked whole, then hid the bench. In the closet. Under some tablecloths. James. The Eagle Scout. But let him tell you what happened next:

"A moment of inattention, and I broke the thing. And then to cover it up! A voice in me kept saying, *See? You're not good enough to be here.* It's all I thought about all day. That evening they had to bring in a chair from the kitchen for the pianist. I slumped down in my seat. Afterwards, as I went back to help clean the room, our teacher was walking toward me, on his way out. I must've looked pretty deflated because he stopped in front of me. I got up the nerve to tell him what I'd done. I'll never forget what he said. 'I'm so glad you told me. Sometimes people don't tell us, so we don't know. Now we can fix it.' His voice was so kind. I worried about this thing all day!

"And then—I never told this to anyone—he raised up the heel of his hand. Gave one smack to my chest. And went on his way. It freaked me out. And I was different for a long time after that. Everything looked different. I walked around for the next four hours like I was in another country. I sat outside under the stars. A light streaked across the sky, then burst, like fireworks.

"No way could I go to bed. Two a.m., I'm sitting in the men's room, watching my feet turn blue from the cold."

Ed. Note: I'm not sure you want to include this story because some guru-wannabe copycat may start hitting people in the chest. I've heard of instances of a master doing such things to awaken a pupil. But you have to be a master!

For James, it certainly broke the hold of identification. Sounds like he was walking around conscious that night.

Sea Change
Margaret, 64, from Fort Lauderdale

Margaret had a few hours before an appointment with her analyst. (Being treated for…?) Time to swim laps. Too many broad-brimmed gals standing around in the pool—late-morning tittle-tattle—but the ocean looked inviting. It was calm that day, the waves smaller than usual.

Here's how Margaret tells it:

"I decided to go in. The Atlantic in January. Ice-cold! Water so freezing cold there's not a thought in my head except to swim as fast as I can. Sooo cold." (Ah! Being treated for cryophobia.)

"Afterwards, I sat on a bench by the beach. Palm trees. Blue sky. Water bright green in the sunlight. Psychedelic." (She was at Woodstock.) "Breeze on my face. Listening to the waves. It was bliss." (Endorphins kicking in.)

"I phoned my therapist to reschedule. I didn't want to talk. I just wanted this. Sitting on that bench. The same in me as in the ocean. Already in paradise."

Ed. Note: As psychiatrist Maurice Bucke might say (his classic book is "Cosmic Consciousness"—have you read it?), something indeed happened in this case, although we may not know exactly what. Enlightenment on that bench? The enlightening activity of attention, perhaps. For Margaret coming awake, it was a matter of: why think about other things now? All around, the extraordinary

Already in paradise

beauty of nature—and a greatness "whose dwelling is the light of setting suns, and the round ocean and the living air." The joy of it, to belong to it, the same quality in oneself.

The Arrival
Jenny, 22, from Westport

Jenny hated to be late. She was sorry that she accepted a ride with the others on their way up to the yoga center in the Catskills. She couldn't tell this driver to hurry. Everyone in the car wanted to stop for coffee, then food. Here's how she described it:

"It was my first retreat—and with a yoga world luminary!" (A what?) "The car ride was taking so long. My stomach was jumpy. I wanted to get there early, to get a good bed in the dorm, because that's what my mother told me to do, and she knows about this kind of thing because she—" (Yes, yes, Jenny, we don't care. Fast-forward, please.) "... got lost! We drove around for an hour and no one could tell us how to—" (Find the place? It's *Deliverance* up there. Better let me tell it. I know when to use "scene" and when to use "summary.")

It was dusk when Jenny wheeled in her Tumi. Bed assignments were already done. People milled around. The woman in charge pointed her toward a somewhat decrepit dormitory farthest from the main building. (It's where they put the young ones.

With the Tumis.) But all the beds were already taken. Except this one spot, in a loft, accessed by a ladder. Not even a bed. A thin piece of foam on a shelf about two feet wide, right on the edge of the opening where the ladder came up. Think *couchette*. But Jenny was horrified: "How could I sleep there? All night I'd be afraid to roll over and fall off."

So Jenny went back to the main house. By this time, everyone was seated in the large hall for the Welcome Meeting. Too tired to sit spine-straight on the floor, Jenny sat on a chair at the back. As she described it, "Everyone looked so old, really old, experienced—way older than me." ("Old hands," as they say. Emphasis on "old.") Jenny wanted to go home. She thought about calling her mother. But then—I'll let her finish it—

"The head yoga instructor came in and began to speak. She was beautiful!" (A reason to stay!) "Even more than in her pictures. So reassuring, that smile. And her voice, the way it made me listen.

"She said, 'I'm happy to see everyone. We've all had a long day, frustrating at times. Just let that be.' Then she gave a guided meditation. The atmosphere in the room changed. I saw it in people's faces. Everyone relaxed. Everything got lighter.

"All of a sudden I wasn't tired anymore. I didn't care at all about earlier—I was just so glad to be in that room. How many people get the chance to work with someone like this?

"And I realized, there was nowhere else on earth I wished to be."

Ed. Note: In the presence of this teacher, Jenny relaxes, focuses her attention, and a shift occurs (as you would say, from reactive mode to receiving mode). It energizes her. She is free from what she'd been thinking. That this happens on her first night, and she feels grateful, bodes well for her.

Salmon Goes Over Falls, Swims Upstream
Murphy, from New York

On the phone a loved one talks about doing something dangerous. I take the bait. I'm against it, and that makes our "discussion" stink like day-old fish. (Sweatin' it!) I'm floundering on the hook, unable to think fast enough for the right thing to say. (Sweaty palms!) The sinker: knowing I'm not being heard, and the feeling of helplessness that goes with it. (Sweat bullets!) There's an inkling that it all may be exaggerated in my fear-rattled brain. (Sweat pants!) But no matter. Over the falls, into toxic waters. And who can swim in sulfuric acid?

I hang up the phone. I feel ill. The one ray of light: remembering to observe myself at least— because something in me still believes it can fix, fix, fix. Call back now? Like a badger at midnight. But sometimes the door has shut tight. (Watch.) Now what? (Watch.) Register my facial expression, the set of the jaw, my abdominal muscles held like this, the set of the shoulders. The mind keeps going back to the problem; the stomach tightens. (Watch.) Even to write down what's going on in my body brings easing. That's the blessing: knowing enough to let it be and just watch until the clouds clear. Through the fog, a little light enters. The hook loosens. Into the glow, even. Does the issue reappear? Sure it does. Right in the pit of my stomach. And the light—is it there, too?

Ed. Note: How remarkable when one can wake up in the midst of an intense identification ("swim in sulfuric acid"). It's a very great thing. It comes with a daily practice. And when there appears (as you call it) a blazing up of consciousness, it's not even about "accepting" anything: for the moment, the blazing up is all.

Are there more instances you can include here, perhaps in less charged circumstances?

Dining In
Murphy, from New York

At a dinner party, I take another forkful. Tasty. I am listening to the others make conversation. The weather tomorrow, plans for the weekend. Mundane. And wonderful. Ordinary is wonderful. I know I am present. I take in the words, the voices, the faces, yes, but even more, the light behind the eyes. How to put it? A tender life there, seen only when I am awake.

The Crossing
Murphy, from New York

Walking briskly on the sidewalk at rush hour, I come upon granny-with-a-cane. No way around her, in the crush of people. It's frustrating, having to hold back. At the corner, both of us stop and wait for the light. Soon I'll have plenty of room to be on my way.

Cars whiz by. I take a few breaths. Become collected—may as well—while waiting. The air feels cool on my skin. Quite a beautiful day, actually. How fast these cars move—it's the Indy 500—and they don't slow down for anything, even the yellow light. Don't dare step off the curb—

The cars stop. The "Walk" sign comes on.

I hear myself say, "Let me help you cross." I offer my arm; she accepts.

As we walk, she mentions she just had a hip operation. I mention that before she steps off the curb she must always check to be sure all the cars have stopped. She agrees. It's like I'm helping my mother across the street. It feels just that way.

Ed. Note: It's striking, how one can be self-centered one moment and centered in Self the next. One begins to awaken and becomes sensitive to one's surroundings. One notices what is needed and just does it. Mother or a stranger, here is a human being needing one's care.

What New World Awaits

Can it be? The shift we are seeing at times, in ourselves and others. Old mind receding. Something new in our way of being alive.

Picture this:

• At any moment, freedom

• All things unnecessary drop away

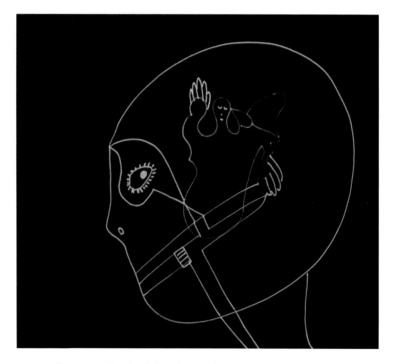

• No longer fooled for long by any voice

• No words separate us from our nature or each other

• Companions together in pure attention

• Grateful for the love of waking up

• People waking, uplifting life on earth

- To really see and know myself well

- Having intention without expectation

- Even when there are pulls, persisting in presence

- Coming into the silence

- Talking and laughing with a friend awake

- No need for another time or place

- Home in an instant

- Filled each second with Attention

- What we wish for is here now

CHAPTER 10

Metamurphosis

Once upon a time there was a sensitive little caterpillar living in a forest. All there was to do all day was eat leaves. Eat leaves and taste things with his feet. But it was a harsh existence. Others were always trying to chew him up.

One day, the eating stopped. He realized he was imprisoned. Unable to move. Hanging upside down. Spun round and bound tight in a cocoon of his own making. The casing was so thick (so as to protect him, he thought) that nothing could penetrate. And even though he wanted to shed those layers, more would form.

He hoped desperately not to fall into that pile of slugs on the ground below and be mistaken for one of them!

He hung on. Through wind and rain. Day and night.

And then it happened. He heard something.

A bird close by. A call he had never heard before. A new thought occurred to him: *Am I dreaming I'm a bug hanging by a thread?* Each note of the song awakened something in him, calling him to another kind of life. The more his listened, the more he wanted that rare bird to become his teacher, wanted to become his pupa, not realizing that he already was; that this was a connection formed over millennia of lifetimes and life forms. But because, at the moment, he didn't have eyes to see, only stemmata, he didn't know where the call was coming from. *Above* was all he knew.

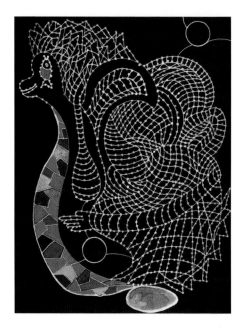

That rare bird

And it was the sweetest song! It went deep into his heart, and he noticed after a while that things were starting to happen inside. Big changes.

Becoming what I am

Every day he listened. Every day the bird came and sang nearby. It was so fine! Such a fine vibration!

And then, one day, the bird flew away.

The branch shook in the wind. The cocoon began to break open. It was magic. He had been transformed! The birdsong had been the kiss of Life, and now he could shed his armor, let it all go, and emerge into the light, beautifully, gloriously free, as he was meant to be.

And as the sun shone in the heavens, the cocoon opened fully. And inside—ah!—

Nothing.

• • •

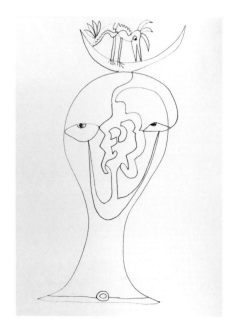

Murphy here.
So that's my little
tale.

The best help for waking up is to be with some-one who is awake. But that's another story.

If I have offended, please excuse. The-One-Who-Thinks-He-Knows couldn't resist removing a few specks from the carpet. Roll it up and put it away.

I love waking up and respect all who wish to wake up, no matter who, how, where, or why. And I am totally grateful to all the beings who came before, who are handing us the keys to the kingdom.

My state has changed—many times—but I'm still here.

Thank you for putting up with me while on this earth.

Ed. Note: About the fable, one expects a butterfly and gets "Nothing"—but a "Nothing" that feels like a Something, sacred, a mystery. It's all unknown, yet one trusts the unfolding. Always fresh, always new.

As you have described it, waking up is a process of discovery, recognizing the finer energy in oneself and embodying it consciously, letting it come into the world.

And perhaps an even higher energy comes.

My Father's House Has Many Mansions

Searching for your place in this world? Hungry to come home? Here are the most helpful guides to today's real estate market for the mindful.

The Hero with a Thousand Houses
　　By Joseph Gambrel

Energy-conscious residences for the elite who have mastered the Spiritual Laws of Abundance. Spacious, glittering, timeless. Country estates in the Cotswolds. Luxe mega-mansions in Makealotakala. Porker-cochon entrances. Prada guard house. Full-page color photos of sensational properties, priced for conspicuous consumption from $100MM. *moneymeansnothingtome.com*

Condos for Consciousness
　　By Dev L. Loper

The complete listing of the world's highest-level

buildings for the spiritually advanced, including The Masters, Mystic Place, VIPassana, The Canaan Grand, Christelle, and The Rapture Beach Club. Close to all the best esoteric schools. 5 BR, 4 bath. Pre-construction prices from $90M. All gold only. *penthouseparadise.com*

The House of Seven Gratefuls
By Bee Holden

Uncover the spiritual solution to every problem: move to Gratitude House. Located in London's ripping Spittlefields district, apartments here are tailored to the different enneagram personality types, including the Professor, the Balabusta, the Basketcase, the Self-Flagellator, the Exhibitionist, the Wallflower, the Toxin, the Ragdoll, and the Failed Actor. Yet in this new environment, all come together in Gratitude! 1-3 BR, 2 bath. *gratefulnests.com*

Getting Into a Gateless Community
By Shamba Lalaland and Hugh Topia

Living alone in the basement of Bleak House? Looking for the stairway to the House of Mirth? Check out this updated list of intentional communities in the land of Nod. Plus, learn what you'll need to bring and do to be accepted, including all about hair shirts, hammers, quinoa, waterboarding, planning meetings, and the rack. *maggiesfarmtwintribesecovillages.com*

Men Are for Cars, Women Are for Castles
By Li'l Squire Footage

Men like to keep moving; women like to nest. This catalogue's ingenious RVs allow Yin and Yang to motor together in style to all the hot chi points, Sedona, Salem, Salt Lake City, Mt. Shafted, and the Northeast Kingdom. For him, a miniature man-cave complete with flat screen and keg holder; for her, a cushy closet with virtual-reality headset featuring digital palace interiors with enormous kitchens. From $99K. *upwardlymobilehomes.com*

No One I Think Is in My Tree House
By Juan Linden

Imagine. Residing 24/7 in a tax shelter of your own making. O, sanctuary! Traditional houses of worship got you down? Build your own. On a boat, up a tree, in your car. Get tax-exempt status by using the secret online name generator, guaranteed to set you up with your own impressive moniker, such as Ho Chi Om Divine Laughter Mission, or Integral Potluck Interfaith Forum, or even Joe's Temple of Light. "One thing I can tell you is it got to be free." *entitled2scamyou.com*

Change Your Dome, Change Your Life
By Geo D. Zak and Iggy Lou

Forget the "old-energy" houses of bricks and mortar. "Dome-iciles" are the Way of the future. These tips for living in your head will change how you live in your head. Over 50 ways to make your skull the best place to dwell, including such chapters as "Trash the Ego and Dance the Tao in Your Head," "Do More By Doing Less in Your Head," and "Cotton Batting Between the Ears." No thoughts, no problems! *majordomo.com*

Heal the Winded Child Within:
Top Exoteric Retreats
By Ko Ann Salon

Don't want to "own"? Find short-term transcendence at rental rates at these Top Eight "best-of" bodhi-work locations: Bed Springs Gone Zendo at Mount Tremperpedic; Land of the Laughing Goatherd Assembly; Donna Helga's Glowing Lizard Yoga Cabinas; Hibachi Temple of Sizzle; Playa Maya Paradisus Butterfly Sanctuary; The Naranjo Ferry; Estelle Freedman's Ordinary Mind Big Mind No Mind Guest House; Vsdlkjijdlkfakra Clksipjtisvara American Center. Hippie expats, indigos, UFO seekers, weekend backpackers—all are welcome. Now in sesshin! *smileatthemosquitoes.com*

MURPHY
xlvii

47 Drawings of
The Wind at Midnight

EXHIBITION CATALOGUE

SOUL PLACE GALLERY
NEW YORK